THE
JOINT CUSTODY
HANDBOOK

THE
JOINT CUSTODY
H A N D B O O K

Creating Arrangements
That Work

. . . .

BY

MIRIAM **G**ALPER **C**OHEN

RUNNING PRESS
Philadelphia, Pennsylvania

Copyright © 1991 by Miriam Galper Cohen.
All rights reserved under the Pan-American and International Copyright
Conventions.

*This book may not be reproduced in whole or in part in any form or by
any means, electronic or mechanical, including photocopying, recording,
or by any information storage and retrieval system now known or
hereafter invented, without written permission from the publisher.*

Canadian representatives: General Publishing Co., Ltd.,
30 Lesmill Road, Don Mills, Ontario M3B 2T6.

International representatives: Worldwide Media Services, Inc.,
115 East Twenty-third Street, New York, NY 10010.

9 8 7 6 5 4 3 2 1
The digit on the right indicates the number of this printing.

Library of Congress Cataloging-in-Publication Number 90–53226

ISBN 0–89471–869–X

Cover design by Toby Schmidt
Interior design by Stephanie Longo
Cover photograph: © J. Taposchaner 1989/PFG International
Author photograph: Joan C. Meyers.
The chart on pages 131–132 originally appeared in "Joint Custody: Is It
Good for the Children?" by Sarah Glazer in *Editorial Research Reports*,
February 3, 1989, and is used with permission.

Typography by Commcor Communications Corporation,
Philadelphia, Pennsylvania
Printed in the United States by Port City Press

This book may be ordered by mail from the publisher. Please add $2.50
for postage and handling. *But try your bookstore first!*

Running Press Book Publishers
125 South Twenty-second Street
Philadelphia, Pennsylvania 19103

G 3 1 1 0 4

Dedication

For the children

Acknowledgments

I am extremely grateful for the participation of many joint-custody families—both parents and children—who shared their experiences with me. They all know the difficulty of attempting to build new lives after divorce and to create two homes where there once was one. Their stories are sometimes painful, sometimes uplifting, and always moving. I sincerely thank them all.

Lawrence Teacher, the publisher of Running Press, recognized the need for the first book about joint custody 12 years ago, and he realized the need for this updated version. He has given me a unique opportunity of being able to revise and refine my thinking about joint custody—a rare experience for an author. I am most thankful.

The editorial staff at Running Press—Nancy Steele, Chris Bittenbender, and especially Greg Aaron—were most helpful.

I thank my agent, Jane Dystel, who persevered so that this book would become a reality.

I am most appreciative of the contributions made to this book by my colleagues and friends, who took the time to share their knowledge with me. In particular, Paula Rosen shared her personal and professional experience with me. Carolyn Kott Washburne contributed her editorial expertise, her enthusiasm, and support. I am indebted to them both.

And finally, once again, my deepest thanks to my family— Herb, Josh, Satya, Jeff, Nicandra, Sarah, and my parents, Charlotte and Sirol Katz—whose love has always sustained me.

Contents

Introduction

Divorce is a painful process—ask anyone who has gone through it. People remember the early years of their separations as being the most difficult time of their lives. Children, too, recall how sad they were when their parents first told them about their divorces. These times brought feelings of profound loss and anxiety. New routines, different schedules, and most likely, new living arrangements contributed to the confusion.

When I wrote my first book on joint custody, *Co-Parenting: Sharing Your Child Equally* (1978), joint custody was a new and controversial concept. During the 1980s, joint custody became a more popular, if controversial, option for families of divorce, with many states enacting joint custody legislation. The transition from having two homes instead of one, while always cumbersome, was difficult in some families and more manageable in others.

In 1978, I naively thought that almost all divorced families could have joint custody and handle it well. I thought that children could easily learn to live in two homes, that even parents who didn't get along could learn to cooperate, and that the benefits that joint custody brings to children—two loving, involved parents— would outweigh any disadvantages. I now see that this is often not the case. While some ideas that I wrote about still hold true today, I have learned that some children never do adjust to moving back and forth between two homes. Some parents continue their battles long after their divorce decree is signed and joint custody becomes an arena for bitterness and constant struggle.

Other families, however, learn to make joint custody work. This book is about what circumstances make joint custody succeed in some instances and fail in others. It is about the variations in joint custody arrangements, the tips and techniques that families have learned over the years to make joint custody easier for everyone, and how to know if joint custody is a good parenting plan for your family.

The motivation for choosing joint custody varies. Some parents feel it will accommodate their work schedules. In other families, neither parent really wants responsibility for raising the children and so joint custody is the least burdensome alternative. Some men think that having joint custody will lower their support payments. Some women agree to joint custody because they fear costly court battles in which they might lose custody altogether. In many families where there is a genuine concern and interest for what's best for the children, joint custody is seen as a way to provide the children with an ongoing, close relationship with both parents.

Whatever the motivation, joint custody is an extremely complex living situation. Like having children, you usually don't know what you're getting into until you do it—and by then, it's too late. Children can't be returned. Many parents report that they had no idea how complicated joint custody and shared parenting would be until they actually began living it, day by day. They then realize how intertwined their lives continue to be with their ex-spouses, how painful it is to be separated from their children even for a few days, and how unwieldy the whole situation can sometimes seem.

But joint custody arrangements, unlike having children, need not be permanent and, in many families, do not last forever. There should be flexibility in the plan and an understanding that modifications can be made in the schedule to suit the changing needs of children and parents. In some families, a schedule is established and remains the same until the children leave home. For most families, however, the parenting plan changes several times as the years go on. Remarriage, a possible move by one parent, and the child's preferences as he or she gets older are just some of the variables which may effect joint custody.

My original book was written from my own co-parenting experiences and those of people I interviewed. Now, 12 years later, I continue to share my own personal experiences and, in as many cases as possible, I went back to interview many of the people I spoke with 12 years ago. Like me, they have learned a great deal with the passage of time and have a perspective on joint custody that now spans many years. My own perspective has been enriched by my work as a family therapist, specializing in work with families in transition. My clients have contributed greatly to my understanding of the process of divorce in general and working out joint custody arrangements in particular.

Throughout the book, you will find quotes from people I have interviewed—friends, clients, friends of friends and professionals in the fields of law and mental health. I have used first names only to identify the genders of the people I spoke with and, except for the professionals, all names have been changed. I hope their experiences will be helpful to you as you consider your own parenting plan. I have alternated using the pronouns *he* and *she*. I have also used the terms *ex-spouse* and *ex-partner* interchangeably to show the difficulties that both mothers and fathers encounter when their marriage dissolves. I have made reference to many books and articles throughout this book. Should you wish further information, you will find these sources listed in the Suggested Readings and Bibliography sections. Professional sources not cited in these sections were interviewed personally.

Joint custody can be viewed as a transition from one family form—the nuclear or intact family—to the divorced or binuclear family, in which the children are members of two households. Through the years, with the parents' commitment to their children's needs as a paramount concern, and with flexibility in the schedule to meet those needs, the children will grow up having a secure, loving relationship with both parents. They can then move out into the world with a strong sense of themselves, ready to take on their own separate lives. Isn't that what all parents— divorced or not—want for their children?

Miriam Galper Cohen
Glenside, Pennsylvania
September, 1990

1

What Is Joint Custody?

Once there was a time when no one had heard of joint custody. Before the 20th century, in the unlikely and unfortunate event of a divorce, fathers were given custody of their children.

Beginning in the early 20th century, courts began to follow the "tender years" doctrine, a policy dictating that young children belong with their mothers. As a result, mothers were granted custody and fathers received minimal visitation rights. There was no big debate about what was best for the children, particularly because divorce seemed so unusual that people didn't think much about it.

Then things seemed to go haywire. The number of women working outside the home increased dramatically, as the second wave of the women's movement hit America in the late 1960s and early 1970s. It was exciting, if threatening, to consider changing the basic assumptions women and men had about themselves and each other. The threatening part was in knowing that for changes to occur, the power relationships between men and women would have to shift. And there were no guarantees about how it would all turn out. A woman who had total responsibility for childrearing would have to relinquish some control in this area if she really wanted her partner to become an active parent. The reward, on the other hand, would be in gaining a true partner to help rear the children.

Women encouraged their husbands to be more involved with the children. Greater involvement by fathers allowed women some child-free time within their marriage—the chance to go back to school, pursue career goals, and be something in addition to wife and mother. Participation by fathers also allowed women to feel that they were supported, both physically and emotionally, in the demanding job of childrearing.

Women working outside the home and fathers changing diapers—this was certainly not the way things had always been done. The move away from traditional roles in conventional marriages upset the balance of power in many relationships. It was difficult for many couples to establish a new dynamic that over-turned the concept of woman's dependence and man's dominance. And so, we began to hear more about divorce. The divorce rate skyrocketed. Divorce became a household word! It was no longer acceptable for people to live in lifeless, loveless marriages.

Every family seemed to be touched in some way by the now-familiar set of circumstances which ripped families apart. Parents began to look for alternatives to traditional custody arrangements. When couples who had shared responsibility for childrearing divorced, neither parent was willing to become a non-custodial parent. Some fathers, as well as mothers, wanted full custody of their children and agreed to share the children as a way to avoid major court battles. Words such as *joint custody, shared parenting,* and *co-parenting* started to appear in print. But what did these words really mean? Did parents really want to split the children in

· · · · · · · · · ·

two, so that Mom wasn't the only one caring for the children? It seemed ridiculous to shuttle the children back and forth between two homes.

In the spring of 1978, I appeared on "The Phil Donahue Show," as it was then called, to discuss the first book on this subject, *Co-Parenting: Sharing Your Child Equally, A Source Book for the Separated or Divorced Family* (Running Press, 1978). The audience thought the idea was preposterous. Share the children? Members of the audience were hostile and outspoken in their view that children belonged with their mothers, period. They spoke up to claim fathers were inept and didn't know how to take care of their own children, especially if a child happened to get sick. To many people, it was somehow un-American for a mother not to want to be with her child 24 hours a day, seven days a week.

Joint custody, co-parenting, shared parenting—this was not an idea whose time had come. The idea was met with anger and fear. Some fathers could not imagine having time to take care of their children. Their priority had always been to earn money, to provide for the family. How could they continue to do that and take care of their children, too? They might have wanted to be more involved with their children, but their lack of knowledge and expertise in parenting made them anxious and fearful about this new role. Men who had not had close contact with their children wondered how they would manage.

The notion of sharing responsibility for children threatened many mothers who saw childrearing as their exclusive responsibility. If they were not actively mothering, then they were at a loss as to their purpose in life. A woman's identity was usually connected with her roles as wife and mother, so when her marital status changed, motherhood seemed to be the only familiar hold on reality.

A woman who has seen herself primarily as a wife and mother and who suddenly has no husband and no children to care for has to come face to face with questions of her own identity and self-worth. If there's no bath to give, no homework to check, no questions to answer (even the ones that previously seemed inane and repetitive), then how would a mother fill her time? There would be no structure for the days, and especially the lonely nights. The anxiety that women feel when they no longer have wifely and motherly duties to carry out, even for a short period of time, can be terribly frightening. These feelings can be just as intense for a mother who has been working outside the home.

Many women were angry at men who, before divorce, showed little interest in their children, but who suddenly wanted to be involved with their children's care. They also were concerned that fathers who were emotionally unfit to be parents were using the banner of joint custody to assume less financial responsibility. Child support is often reduced if a father takes care of his children half or part of the time, although a mother without an income of her own still has to depend on the support to pay the rent and feed the children.

Most lawyers and judges were not in the forefront of promoting change in custody arrangements. For the most part, they maintained the old order—custody to the mother, visitation for the father (the "tender years" doctrine). Dustin Hoffman's portrayal in the 1979 film *Kramer vs. Kramer* of a distraught, divorced man who had to battle in court for his right to be an active father to his son brought the issue to the fore.

During the early 1980s, more divorcing parents became interested in sharing responsibility for raising their children, although they were still a minority of divorcing parents. They worked out schedules for their children and did their best to stay out of each other's way while maintaining an active parenting partnership. The courts became interested too—almost to the point of viewing joint custody as a cure for the problems custody issues presented to divorcing families. It was almost as if the courts felt they could insist that parents cooperate, that they could legislate good will between parents at war with one another. State after state adopted various forms of custody legislation, some making joint custody a presumption, the first arrangement considered. Joint custody legislation began to appear in most states.

New research was published about the long-term effects of divorce upon children. Research showed that what happened between parents in the years after a divorce had more impact on children than the relationship between parents before the divorce. Also, children who had the most successful adjustment to a divorce were those who had continuous close contact with both parents. This seemed to confirm the belief of those who thought that joint custody was the best arrangement for children. If both parents remained actively involved with their children, the theory went, they could each provide their children with separate homes and lives that were calm, well-ordered, and loving.

However, beginning in 1980, professionals began to report different results: lives that were never reordered, and children who, years after their parents' divorces were destroyed psychologically. Many children remained depressed and angry, experiencing difficulty in school and in their own relationships.

New theories were formed on what was best for children, and joint custody arrangements were singled out as the most confusing, the most upsetting, and the most difficult for children. Information about the effects of divorce was becoming as confusing and as conflicting as divorce itself.

To simplify custody arrangements, some people urged a return to the simple tender years doctrine: custody to Mother, visitation rights to Father. Many felt that moving children repeatedly from one house to another, in what was already a difficult situation, was far too much to ask. Others felt that without a continual, close relationship with both parents, a child's emotional development would be stunted. Only a joint custodial arrangement could provide for intense bonding between the child and both parents.

Within a ten-year period, the entire notion of joint custody had become almost as controversial as when it first arrived on the scene. It seemed to be getting more difficult to figure out what was in the best interests of the child.

. . . .

To add to the confusion, terms with similar-sounding names, such as co-parenting, joint custody, and shared parenting had emerged but not been distinguished from one another. Does joint custody mean that the child spends equal amounts of time with each parent? What if parents have joint custody and one parent wants to move away with the children? Who makes such a decision? Should children have a say in where they will live?

What exactly are people talking about when they say they want or have joint custody? Probably several different things. Joint custody has both legal and physical definitions. Legal joint custody means that parents share responsibility for making major decisions about the children. Together, they decide on issues of education, health care, and religious upbringing. In every other way, the agreement may look very similar to a traditional custody arrangement in which the mother has custody and the father has visitation rights.

Physical joint custody means that children live with each parent part of the time—sometimes time is divided equally, and sometimes not. Theoretically, physical joint custody also means that *all* responsibilities and rights of parenthood are shared: all tasks related to childrearing are divided between the parents, and major decisions concerning the health and well-being of the children are made jointly. Some people prefer not to use the term joint custody at all. They prefer "shared parenting," which they feel more clearly denotes how some parents raise their children after divorce.

Split custody means that children are divided between parents— one child lives with one parent, and another child resides with the other parent. Long-distance custody arrangements exist in which a child lives with one parent during the school year and visits with the long-distance parent during holidays and summer vacations.

The variety in custody arrangements seems endless. But it is not the structure of the arrangement that matters most; it is the quality of relationships within the arrangement that makes all the difference.

. . . .

In the best joint-custody arrangements, both parents share the attitude that they are deeply connected to one another through their children and that each respects the other's relationship with those children. Both parents are involved in the daily routines of family life. Both have days when they get up early with their children, pack their lunches, get them off to school, talk to teachers, and drive to piano lessons, as well as days that are designated as play days. Both parents are responsible for taking care of a sick child, for making dentist appointments, for getting prescriptions filled, and for buying new sneakers. These tasks can be divided in some way. What is important is that both parents assume responsibility for meeting a share of all the physical, as well as the financial, emotional, and spiritual needs of their children.

Throughout this book, I will tell you the stories of three families. The first family, the Gordons, created what has come to be called a *binuclear* family. After the divorce, both Gordons remarried and became stepparents, and one began a second family. The two families live near each other, the children move back and forth between the two homes, and the adults are friendly and civil to one another. Holidays and celebrations are shared, and no one is excluded from important events concerning the children of the first marriage. The two interrelated households and one family system are held together by the original couple and their children. The Gordons, and other families like them, are a model of cooperative parenting and joint custody at its best.

A second kind of joint-custody arrangement exists when divorced couples, while holding shared parenting as an ideal, are less interested in maintaining friendly relations. Rather, they remain neutral, speak to each other only when necessary, and lead separate lives. They know that if they were to have more dealings with one another, someone would get upset and the delicate balance they have managed to achieve could be easily dismantled.

The Brewers are an example. Each parent really would have preferred to have had sole custody, but in order to avoid a long, costly court battle, they agreed on legal and physical joint custody. The Brewers have changed their schedules several times over the years to adapt to their children's changing needs, but they rigidly adhere to whatever schedule they have at the moment. The Brewers don't want to be forced to speak with each other, negotiate for time, or in any way deal with each other except when absolutely necessary. Their relationship is businesslike. They speak to each other only on the night before the children make the transition from one home to the other, and they limit their discussion to essentials.

The third family, the Amatos, have a truly troublesome situation. For them, joint custody was ordered by the court, but not because it was the option most likely to work well for both the parents and the children. Rather, joint custody was decided on as a result of a bitter custody dispute which the judge was at a loss to resolve in another way. Neither the bitterness nor the dispute ended with the judge's order.

Beverly Webster Ferreiro, Ph.D., Associate Clinical Professor of Nursing at the University of North Carolina School of Nursing at Chapel Hill, says it is "unthinkable that disputing parents would be awarded joint custody without a clear contractual understanding of how they will carry out their parenting responsibilities." Yet this happens regularly, and there is little hope of ever resolving the discord.

This is precisely what has happened with the Amato family. The children live with their mother on Monday, Tuesday, and Wednesday, and go to school from her house. On Thursday afternoons, they are picked up by their Dad, who lives half an hour away, and stay with him through Monday morning. (He drives them to and from school on Fridays.) The parents have never calmed down; their fury at each other is as intense as the day they divorced, and they are open about it with the children.

Arguments continue over small issues like the children's participation in sports—which Little League, which soccer team. Or Dad may think he has worked out extended vacation plans with the children according to the dictates of the court order when Mom vetoes the trip at the last moment and threatens to have the police at his door if he doesn't return the children promptly. This situation is not what was intended in the original notion of co-parenting.

Legally, these parents have joint custody, but there is no spirit of agreement. These parents, as Isolina Ricci notes, are "unable or unwilling to discuss the children's needs with each other, and their communications are strained or nonexistent. The parents will only contact one another in emergencies or in case of illness." This relationship is what Ricci and others call *parallel parenting*.

The Gordons, the Brewers, and the Amatos all have joint custody. Some agreements are of their own making, and others were made for them. Their stories illustrate how similar joint-custody arrangements may look from the outside, but how different they may be in day-to-day life. The common thread is that the children go back and forth between two homes on a regular basis, but the quality of relationships between ex-spouses and the adjustment of the children after divorce varies considerably.

Another family you will read about is my own. It seems so long ago that my ex-husband and I separated. Jeff and I were married in August, 1965, when he was 23 and I was 25. Joshua was born in January, 1970. Jeff and I separated in February, 1974. We were divorced in May, 1976.

The chronology seems cold and doesn't reveal that after all these years, we are still family. We no longer live in the same community—Jeff and his wife, Nicandra, live in Vermont with their baby, Sarah; I live in Philadelphia with my husband, Herb, and stepdaughter, Satya; and Josh is away at college in Connecticut—yet there is a bond between us that the years have not weakened. Jeff and I shared childrearing activities fairly equally from the time we separated, when Josh was four years old, until Josh moved with Jeff to Vermont, when he was 14. Josh divided his time between our two homes. We lived close to one another and planned our separate lives so that we could be

. . . .

effective co-parents. We cooperated on all matters concerning Josh's upbringing, and our commitment to remain active parents never wavered.

Legally, I had sole custody. That was suggested by my lawyer, who told me that a judge would never approve joint custody. Jeff didn't have a lawyer of his own, and he accepted the recommendation of my lawyer. We wrote our own separation agreement, which my lawyer looked over. All in all, it was a fairly benign process. Our feelings about separating were not benign, and Josh's reaction to our separation was anything but favorable, but our desire to share equally in the joys and responsibilities of parenting was never questioned. It was just a matter of what kind of arrangements we would make for Josh.

In the early years of our co-parenting agreement, Jeff and I consulted each other regularly. It seemed that we were continuously working out arrangements, talking about Josh's reactions to our separation, anticipating his needs, settling financial accounts, and dealing with our own feelings about how much contact we were having with each other—at the same time that we were working on distancing ourselves from one another. As the years went by, we all became fairly accustomed to our routines. My relationship with Jeff was based on mutual respect and trust, and a feeling that it would be best for Jeff and I to nurture our relationship with a maximum of goodwill and a minimum of conflict.

Some thought we were pioneers participating in a noble experiment in living. Some people said it couldn't be done, that we were fooling ourselves and confusing Josh by not having clearer boundaries between us. If we could celebrate holidays together and if we were so friendly, then why weren't we still married? I can still hear the questions, so many years later.

In any case, we had divorced, and the divorce was final. Josh's needs changed along with ours as we entered new relationships and moved forward with our lives. Not written into the agreement, but clearly understood by both of us, was that whoever moved away from Philadelphia moved without Josh. No one moved—not for ten years, anyway. The possibility did come up at various times prior to the ten-year mark, but it was too painful to think of leaving Josh, so neither of us did.

Jeff subsequently decided to move to Vermont, and, after much deliberation and family discussions, Josh decided to move with him. So there I was, the parent with sole custody, suddenly becoming a long-distance parent. I held on to the fact that Jeff and I had succeeded in being partners in parenting over the years, and to the belief that somehow I would be able to continue the same kind of involvement with Josh, although not on a day-to-day basis. Jeff and I still considered ourselves co-parents and I still had a lot to say in how Josh was being raised, although now I'd have to say it from a distance and make sure my voice was heard.

For a variety of reasons, many children who have been raised in two homes after divorce choose to live with one parent, usually the same-sex parent, when they become teenagers. They want one phone number, one closet, and as much a sense of normalcy as they can get. When this happens, whether it's a move that involves long distances or one that is just around the corner, the separation can feel equally painful to a parent.

Some people react to a teenager's desire to live in one home after living in two for many years as a rejection of joint custody. If joint custody were such a success, they reason, then the child would continue living in two homes until she goes off to college and establishes her own, independent life. I don't view it that way. Joint custody can be successful until the child's needs change, or until a parent remarries, moves away, or has more babies. What is successful for one period in a family's life may need to be reevaluated later on.

As a family therapist specializing in working with families in transition, I have seen, truly, the best and the worst of people who are divorcing. It is inspiring to be with those parents who want to do the best thing for their children, who are willing to stop blaming each other and accept equal responsibility for their family life. On the other hand, parents who cannot seem to reduce the hatred they feel for their ex-spouses and who want only revenge inflict serious psychological damage on themselves and their children. Meanwhile, the children either make their peace and adapt to their new living arrangements or become endlessly involved in their parents' battles. In either case, they experience a great deal of pain, anger, and sadness at the changes in their lives. Throughout this book, you will read about families who have successful joint custody arrangements and those for whom joint custody has been a total failure that made victims of innocent children.

I hope you will see yourself in the pages of this book—in the stories of couples struggling to free themselves from a destructive marriage yet still trying to be good parents to their children, and even in the stories of parents who are angry and resentful about the hand that's been dealt them. This book is for parents trying to learn, from the experiences of others, whether joint custody is best for their children and for themselves.

2

Spouses No Longer, Parents Forever

There have been times when I truly wished he had been run over by a truck. There were times when he wanted things his way and I wanted them my way. On balance, though, there are a lot worse guys I could have had a child with. We've both worked hard to keep the lines of communication open between us, knowing that in the long run, that would be best for our daughter. [Charlotte]

Many divorced parents I know have wished, at one time or another, that their former partner would die. These fantasies usually are fairly well developed: a car wreck, a plane crash, a heavy object falling from a tall building. Milder forms of these fantasies include the disappearance of a former spouse rather than a violent death. The more difficult and bitter the divorce, the greater the rage and anger at the former spouse, and the more likely it is that these fantasies will flourish.

For most people, however, these fantasies are fleeting. Even though the death of their former spouse would mean that they would have the children all to themselves and would no longer have to discuss an arrangement, negotiate a schedule, or argue about how some childrearing matter is handled, most divorced parents recognize the importance the other parent plays in their lives and in the lives of their children.

Most divorced parents want to be responsible parents, and understand that their children's relationship with both parents is important. Even in the midst of open warfare, most divorcing parents will admit that they want their children to have a good relationship with the other parent. It seems common knowledge now that children need to be close to both parents, wherever they live. One loving parent is good; two are better. Two parents—who can both provide a child with unconditional love, delight in the child's accomplishments and cute little remarks, and share in the child's sorrow—are better than one.

In their book *Surviving the Breakup*, Judith S. Wallerstein and Joan Berlin Kelly discuss the importance of children maintaining contact with both parents. Their five-year study of children of divorce identifies the quality of the relationship with *both* parents as one of the most significant factors in a child's healthy adjustment to divorce. Findings regarding the centrality of both parents to the psychological health of children and adolescents alike lead many experts to hold that, where possible, divorcing parents should be encouraged and helped to shape postdivorce arrangements which permit and foster continuity in the children's relations with both parents.

Suppose you accept the wisdom of the professionals. How are you going to put their ideas into practice? It's one thing to want your child to have a relationship with his other parent. But what about you? What kind of position does that put you in? If you have had a bitter divorce, the last thing you want is to discuss your child's daily life with your ex-mate. Or suppose you and your former mate still like each other quite a bit and you actually enjoy the frequent contact you have, ostensibly to talk about the kids. Some divorced couples know that if they speak to each other too much, the delicate balance of neutrality they have managed to create will tumble. So they deliberately keep their distance.

Dr. Marla Isaacs, co-author of *The Difficult Divorce*, describes three kinds of postdivorce relationships: friendly, neutral, and hostile.

Friendly Relations

Friendly parents are those who can cooperate easily regarding the needs of their children.

The conversations of these parents are marked by a spirit of cooperation and goodwill. Their stance toward one another is to be helpful and to encourage and promote the relationship they each have with their children. To serve the needs of the children, any bitterness and jealousy are set aside. Friendly parents can celebrate important events in the child's life together, such as birthdays and holidays. Very often, these events also include grandparents from each side of the family. Everyone can gather for a high-school graduation, and the atmosphere, while somewhat uncomfortable, is at least not tense. Relations are, for the most part, harmonious.

The Gordons are a good example of friendly parents. Naomi and Mark live next door to each other. For the past 11 years, they have followed the same schedule of shared parenting for their two children. Only on special occasions such as vacations and holidays do they alter their routine. Each has remarried, and their new spouses are friendly with each other as well. Naomi and her new husband, Gary, have a child of their own who considers Mark and his new wife part of his family. Mark's wife, Heather, has two children from a previous marriage, and she shares responsibility for raising them with her ex-husband.

When they have issues to talk about concerning their children, Naomi and Mark want to be helpful to one another. They want the best for their children. Their approach is to problem-solve, to come to some meeting of the minds, and to put their plans into action. Certainly, they have had difficult times as parents. During the spring of 1986, as Mark and Naomi's oldest daughter was making plans to attend a summer exchange program for teenagers in Denmark, the first traces of nuclear fallout were detected from the Soviet nuclear disaster at Chernobyl. Naomi wanted to cancel the trip. Mark thought she was overreacting and told her so. They were both upset and it didn't seem that they could reach an understanding. In the end, Naomi did not give in; Mark thought that she was making a big mistake, but their daughter stayed home that summer.

Such disagreements are now rare for the Gordons. They have been friends for many years, they share common values, and they have built on the shared history of their marriage by continuing to share responsibility for their children. They are warm and caring toward each another, and they support and protect the relationship that the other parent has with the children. They have many friends in common, and they participate in the same community activities. Life seems easy for this binuclear family.

Given all this, there still may be bittersweet feelings. Says Naomi,

My children have added two parents, one half brother, and two stepbrothers to their family. They feel enriched by the additional love and fun. It's worked out extremely well, but I would still rather have my children with me all the time.

Neutral Relations

A neutral relationship between ex-partners is characterized by parents who, while they may not like each other, have managed to put aside their bitterness for the sake of the child's best interests.

These parents talk to each other only to take care of business, make arrangements for special events, or in case of an emergency. Neutral parents don't do anything to help or hinder the relationship between them and their children, although they acknowledge the importance of that relationship. They do not feel friendly toward each other, and they are rarely, if ever, moved by feelings of warmth and caring for each other. In order to make their kind of parenting partnership work, they have to stay out of each other's way as much as possible.

Sally and Vic Brewer divorced five years ago. They knew then, as they do now, that to be effective parents for their three children, they needed to establish a routine and stick to it, no matter what. They don't talk to each other the night before the kids make the transition from one house to the other. They go to parent/teacher conferences separately. They celebrate birthdays separately. Christmas is never a family affair. When their oldest child graduates from high school in a few years, Sally and Vic both will attend the graduation and will probably sit together, but it won't be a very comfortable time for either of them. They lead separate lives, and they like it that way. Says Sally:

We understood we had really different ways of looking at the world and at our children. One thing we've never done, though, is put each other down in front of the kids, and we've never denied each other access to the kids. We may not be friendly, but we've never been cruel, either. I guess we're somewhere in the middle.

When there's a problem to discuss, Sally and Vic do their best to come to a decision quickly. If the conversation were to drift away from the focus of the children's welfare, all their underlying anger and bitterness would surface. To avoid the deeper conflict they still feel with one another, they purposely move to a quick resolution of their discussions.

· · · · · · · · ·

Hostile Relations

A hostile relationship is one in which anger and bitterness mark almost every interaction.

In this relationship, there is little trust or cooperation. These parents would not consider going out of their way for each other, and they speak directly to each other only on rare occasions. The relationship is potentially volatile at every turn; a simple request could turn into a major confrontation. Feelings of rage and the desire for revenge lurk so close to the surface that they could be ignited at a moment's notice. The fact that the children may be present doesn't stop these parents from expressing their hatred for each other.

In this kind of relationship, children are often used as messengers. "You can tell that lying, no-good mother of yours that if she thinks she can order me around anymore, she's dead wrong," says Jack to his little boy.

It is not uncommon for joint custody to be awarded by judges in contested custody cases when parents are at war with each other. In *The Difficult Divorce*, Marla Beth Isaacs, Braulio Montalvo, and David Abelson assert that although both parents may be fit to be parents and both homes suitable for raising children, the atmosphere between the parents is too full of hatred to award joint custody. At best, joint custody can create an impossible situation for the child, who is caught between his parents in a continuing battle. "In a volatile situation, the least favored alternative is to create proximity between the couple. Joint custody would do just that," they believe.

Jack and his ex-wife, Jacqueline, know that their continued hostilities upset their children, yet they cannot seem to interrupt the pattern that has existed since their relationship began. Jack, a client of mine for several years, has learned that it's best to withdraw from the fray and to work toward a relationship of peace and harmony, or at least coexistence.

There are moments, however fleeting, during which Jack feels he is accomplishing his goal. A civil conversation with his ex-wife that lasts for two minutes is a major victory for Jack. He then is moved to do his ex-wife a favor: to pick up the children on a day which is not his, but which makes life easier for Jacqueline. The momentary warm glow is elusive, however; the next interaction he has with Jacqueline is marked by vindictive assaults on him. He admits using the children as messengers—not just for saying cruel things, which he knows he shouldn't do, but for delivering messages about such things as school and doctor's appointments. He simply doesn't want to speak to his ex-wife ever again if he can help it.

Is this an atmosphere in which to raise children? Of course not. Jack, a devoted father, is trying to build a new life for himself and for his children. His new life includes minimal contact with his ex-wife, even though he has custody four days a week and the children are with their mother three days a week. That's a lot of going back and forth and, one would think, a lot to talk about with your parenting partner. But Jack and Jacqueline do not consider themselves partners; they think of themselves as single parents, doing the best they can.

In my work with families in transition, I make it very clear to parents that their relationship is the key to their children's well-being. It always has been and always will be. Just as their relationship during marriage set the tone for their previous family life, so will their postdivorce relationship set the tone for their current family life. I tell them that they are unrealistic if they think that just because they live in separate homes, their relationship will not affect their children. My goal in therapy is to find ways to keep both parents involved in their children's lives and to reduce hostilities.

If seeing the other parent causes flare-ups, then I suggest that the parents arrange transition days so that the children move from one house to the other through neutral territory—school, child care, a neighbor, or a relative. In this case, the way to minimize hostilities is to help the parents avoid seeing each other. If requests to change the routine create animosity, it is then necessary to develop an agreement in which each parent is responsible for the children during his or her own time. Anything and everything should be done to keep hostilities down and to keep both parents involved.

You may wonder how parents who are so angry at each other can sit in the same room. Very often they cannot, and in that case I work with parents individually until the atmosphere has calmed down. A hostile couple has probably already spent a fortune in a custody battle and feels spent emotionally, too. While the idea of sitting in the same room together is unpleasant, the idea of going back to court is even less appealing. In the meantime, their children's well-being is at stake.

Your New Relationship

In *Vicki Lansky's Divorce Book for Parents*, the author advises: "Approach your new relationship with the other parent as a business partnership. You are partners in a business. The assets are your children."

What kind of relationship do you have with your child's other parent? Are you satisfied with this relationship or would you like to see some changes? Make a list for yourself of the positive and negative aspects of your relationship with your ex-spouse. Several books are available that include a series of checklists to help you evaluate your relationship with your ex-partner. Two helpful books are *Sharing the Children* by Robert E. Adler, Ph.D., and *Mom's House, Dad's House* by Isolina Ricci. They discuss issues such as parenting styles, communication, financial negotiations, and conducting business with each other.

Would you describe your dealings with your ex-mate as friendly, neutral, or hostile? At various times in your postdivorce life, your relationship with your ex-spouse probably fits all three categories, perhaps even all three at once.

When we split up, we were furious at each other. We couldn't stand the sight of each other. It's been 16 years now, and a lot has happened in that time, some good, some bad. We did stay friendly enough to raise our son together, and that's been the most important thing. [Molly]

Molly describes a relationship with her ex-husband, Steve, in which the arguments they had during their marriage continued after the marriage was over—specifically about how to raise their son. They argued about discipline, bedtime, cleaning up, permissiveness versus rigidity—in short, about everything. When Molly and Steve separated, they agreed that they'd share in raising their son, Owen, as equally as possible. They worked out a schedule in which Owen was with each of them for equal amounts of time. They could be flexible about timing—one issue that did not lend itself to fighting. As years went by, their arguments about how to raise Owen continued.

"I never gave an inch to Steve," says Molly. "I wanted to protect Owen from what I thought was Steve's harshness. I'd insist on my way. Steve would finally acquiesce and then resent it." They did always talk about Owen, but they seemed to worry about different things. Yet their friendship has endured over the years. She says:

Our main focus as friends was Owen. He was our reason for talking. I was always interested in Steve's life but I would never have called him to talk about that. Now that Owen is out of the house and on his own, I never see or talk to Steve. We'll always be friends, though. We've gone through a lot together and you don't just throw that away.

How much contact should two people who used to be married to each other have? There are no rules. At times you'll want to talk a lot; at other times you'll prefer to avoid contact. When you feel lonely, you might find yourself calling your ex more often, even if

· · · · · · · · · ·

the pretext is to talk about Johnny's problems in school. If you're in the midst of a torrid new love affair, the last thing you might want to do is talk to your ex. Combinations of guilt and joy flood you, and talking to your ex-spouse complicates so many things.

After you first separate, you'll probably experience conflicting needs and emotions and live with opposing, ambivalent feelings. At one moment, you may feel furious at your ex-spouse, and within the same hour feel sad and miss your former mate. You might wish this person would disappear from the face of the earth and then wish your former spouse would come get the children, because you can't take care of anyone right now.

Change is the nature of all relationships, especially those in which emotions are charged. The relationship you have with your ex-spouse, particularly right after a separation, is not a neutral one. It would be a rare couple who could separate one day and have a great deal of trust for each other the next. Feelings of trust develop slowly after a separation, if at all, even though trust may have existed during the marriage.

You need time to pull back, to separate yourself from your ex-spouse, to mourn the loss of the relationship. A period of withdrawal from your ex-spouse is normal and necessary after separating. Some people decide that they want to remain withdrawn and choose to build a new parenting partnership based on neutrality and distance. These people speak to their ex-spouses only when necessary, and they concentrate on being civil. They try not to blame each other but rather look for solutions to their problems.

What was good about your relationship in the past? Says Audrey,

Not much. We always had different values and we always had a tough time talking to each other. The one thing that has lasted is that I've always respected the relationship Walter has with the children. He is a good father and I'm grateful for that.

Audrey and Walter don't have much to do with each other now, and they didn't have much to do with each other when they were married. Both were always concerned about their children, however, and they have continued to be involved parents.

It's natural in this period to deny that anything good ever existed in your marriage. Forging your new identity as a separate person sometimes conflicts with maintaining a civil relationship with your ex-spouse.

Why all this talk about civility? Why bother? Sally and Vic talk about not bad-mouthing the other in front of the children.

"It only comes back to haunt you," says Vic. More importantly, Vic says, he realized that if he called Sally stupid in front of his daughter, then his daughter would feel stupid, too. "I'd never want that to happen," says Vic. "It's easier to just try to act like a human being. That old 'do unto others' thing has carried me through a lot of angry times."

An extremely delicate balance exists in a relationship between two people who are no longer married to each other but remain involved through their children. Two people who want to know what's going on in their children's daily lives yet who need to distance themselves emotionally from each other are going to have a hard time drawing boundaries.

How much talking is too much? One person may feel relieved to be out of an unhappy marriage, and so talking about the children seems relatively painless. The other partner, meanwhile, may feel awful, depressed, and disoriented. Talking about the children is just one more way to stay attached and connected to a person she feels very bitter toward right now. It's difficult to give each other support as parents and at the same time withdraw from each other's emotional lives.

In making arrangements for the children, you may find out that your ex-spouse has a new relationship. You may hear how happy he or she is, how well things are going. You had hoped there would be some remorse, some guilt about leaving you. But no, life looks good. Child care? Alimony? Why would you want to make things even easier for your ex-spouse than they already are? This is a perfect chance for revenge.

It takes time to break habits and to establish new patterns of interacting. It's easy to fall back on the patterns that used to be destructive in your relationship, the ones that made you feel awful about yourself.

For example, perhaps you are a father who has never been generous about money. You always wanted your wife to justify her need for money and to account for almost every penny she spent. The children didn't need such expensive clothes, you would say. They'd only outgrow them anyway. Now that you have both decided to share responsibilities for raising the children, you think she should share in the finances as well—especially since she seems to be enjoying herself so much. Yes, you seem to be getting angry about the same thing all over again—money.

This is not the time to carry on in the same manner. It's time to break old habits, challenge old ways of thinking, and to establish new patterns of interacting. Money is a particularly difficult subject. What you should consider is how your attitudes and your relationship with your ex-wife will serve your children. You may never have liked the way your ex-wife handled money, and you may not like it now, but you have a responsibility to her and to your children to work out a financial arrangement that suits all of you.

New Ways to Communicate

Some people estimate that it takes three to five years for couples to disentangle themselves from their spousal relationship and to establish new modes of interacting, with the children as their focus. If you're newly separated, three to five years might seem like an eternity. Estimates don't always apply to individuals, however. Your pace in sorting out your relationship with your ex-spouse very much depends on how you've managed your relationship until now, and what decisions you can and cannot make together, especially regarding the needs of your children.

. . . .

It may be very confusing at first to figure out how many and what kind of discussions you need to have with each other in order to share parenting tasks. Limiting your initial discussions to business items, such as making new child-care arrangements, will be helpful. Doing this might give you the opportunity to work with each other on a specific task. For example, you could interview sitters together or visit your child's school to talk with the teachers.

The focus of time you spend with each other should be on planning together for your child's needs. *Mom's House, Dad's House* by Isolina Ricci is an excellent sourcebook for parents who want to make joint custody work. Ricci suggests guidelines for negotiations with the other parent, as well as guidelines for business discussions between divorcing parents.

"Choose a meeting time that is best for your partner and yourself," she writes. "Don't make it the end of a long hard day or when you are hungry. Limit your discussion time to 30 minutes. Only cover a few items in one session. Save the difficult topics for later. When you disagree, look for the ways each of you could give in a little." Ricci's ideas are helpful in any negotiation, especially when emotions run high.

Some parents feel they need to stay in almost constant contact in order to discuss their children's needs. In retrospect, many of these parents admit that this was to meet their own needs as well.

"I never wanted to stop talking to my ex-husband," says Roberta. "I loved him then and I love him now. It's just that our marriage didn't work any more."

Roberta and her ex-husband, Ed, noticed that people thought they were not handling their divorce well. During the first six months after their separation, they met for dinner on a regular basis, talked to each other on the phone several times a week, and stayed in close contact regarding their children's reactions to the separation. They were told by friends and relatives that they were seeing too much of each other and that if they really intended to divorce, they were asking for trouble. Ed describes this time as the most difficult period of his life:

· · · · · · · · · ·

I could never just cut off all relations with Roberta. It would be like cutting off my arm. It would be inhuman and unreal to think that I would live with someone for 15 years and then not have anything to do with her. What about the human heart? And what about the kids? We still had kids together and we had to think together about how to raise them and how to love them.

Roberta and Ed gradually decreased the amount of time they spent together. It was becoming too painful. They found that it was more difficult to begin their new lives when they still clung to each other for moral and emotional support. They had to work at letting go of their *spousal relationship* yet continue their *parenting relationship.* They continue to talk with each other several times a week, but they restrict their discussions to scheduling, school work, doctors' appointments, and how the children are getting along. They always talk to each other the night before the children change houses. They want to know what their children's days have been like, what kind of mood they're in, whether anything important has happened, and whether any projects are due at school. They prepare each other for the transition.

You can be a loving parent to your children and assume your share of responsibility without knowing what your children's days have been like with the other parent. There may be times when you really don't care to know how well things have gone at the other house, or how excited your child is about planning a trip with his other parent when you're having trouble making ends meet. You may need more distance from your ex-spouse, and while you know that it's better for the children if you and your ex talk more often, that might be too painful for you to manage at this time.

Whatever relationship you work out with your ex-spouse, your purpose is to continue sharing the responsibilities for bringing up your children. Some people assume that in order to have a successful joint-custody arrangement, parents must view life similarly and raise their children with similar values. Parents living in a nuclear family often disagree about child-rearing, and the children know it, yet no one suggests a divorce. What's important is how differences are handled.

Agreeing to Disagree

Frank tells a funny story about something that was no laughing matter at the time.

Our daughter, Hallie, used to wet the bed at night, and her mother and I used to try to figure out where Hallie peed more—her house or mine. It turned out for whatever reason to be at Barbara's house. Things got serious when Barbara advocated using some machine that goes off when the child pees. It wakes up the whole block, everybody but the kid. It's a water-sensitive pad that sets off a bell when it gets wet. I told Barbara that I didn't want her to use such a horrendous device. She was angry because she had already sent for it and she was sure it would work.

This could have been one of those issues that caused us to flare up for a while, but fortunately it wasn't. Finally, I told Barbara that I would do everything to support her using it at her house. As it turned out, she decided not to use it. Fortunately for the whole neighborhood, Hallie gradually stopped.

Parents have different ideas about appropriate bedtimes, toothbrushing, when homework should be done and in what atmosphere (television on or off, on the living-room floor or in bedrooms with desks, chairs, and lamps). The situations that parents who have joint custody can argue about are unlimited, just as unlimited opportunities exist to handle differences in a mature manner. Joint custody does illuminate the differences.

"I always let Owen stay up as long as he liked," says Molly. "I thought he could regulate his own need for sleep, and besides, I liked his company." Steve, Owen's father, would be furious at Molly when Owen arrived at his home sleepy, saying he had stayed up late to watch an old movie on television:

Molly's idea of discipline was that you don't do it. She never told Owen when to do anything. Discipline was left to me, and I got to be the bad guy. It's a good thing we had joint custody, so Owen would have to brush his teeth at least three or four times a week. Otherwise, they would have all rotted away by now. [Steve]

Molly and Steve used to argue a lot about what they separately viewed as Molly's permissiveness and Steve's hard-line approach. They fought about this when they lived together, and it was no surprise to them that they fought about it afterward. They finally agreed that they would never agree and that each could do as they pleased in their own homes. Owen would have to learn that his parents viewed him and the world differently, and he would have to adjust accordingly. The one thing Molly and Steve had to be aware of was that Owen would try to use these differences to his own advantage. What parent hasn't heard the plaintive remark, "But Mommy lets me...." The answer is straightforward: "Yes, Mommy does let you, but Daddy doesn't."

You can argue the differences and see if you can come to some workable solution, or you can let the differences be, acknowledging that they exist and hoping that your children will adapt as best they can. Charlotte asserts,

Jim and I bend over backwards not to get into squabbles with each other about where and how Julie spends her time. We know several couples who always fight about the kids, about who's going to spend what time with the kids. Just about any issue you name they don't agree on. Jim and I are very careful not to get involved in that. If some point of conflict does come up, such as one night when each thought the other was going to have Julie, or something like that, we'll both defer to the other: you first—no, you first. We don't want to get involved in petty squabbles because it's so destructive. If we did, then everything else would go downhill.

Jeff and I also worked at being gracious, even though the first few years after our separation were marked by feelings of anger and bitterness. Although we said we wanted to be on good terms and thought that would be good for our son, we didn't trust each other very much. Still, for the most part, we were civil to each other. During this initial period of separation, we talked on the phone almost daily. We felt it was important to share Josh's reactions to our separation and the ways we each responded to those reactions. Like Roberta and Ed, we also needed to stay in close contact to meet our own needs. Gradually we became more amicable, and the friendship that had been a strength during our marriage once more came to the forefront of our relationship.

In the 16 years since we separated, Jeff and I have built separate lives, yet have remained actively involved with each other in being parents to our son. There were difficult times, to be sure, but overall, we've been able to solve problems, share in the joys of parenting, and feel proud of the partnership we created and still maintain.

Your relationship with your ex-spouse can take many different forms. Even when you settle into a routine and feel you've established some sense of normalcy, that relationship can change. You can be friendly and communicate with ease, or you can be distant and keep your relationship strictly business. Your goal is to maintain a relationship that doesn't just allow you, but actually encourages you, to be the best parents you can be to your children.

You will always be related to each other through your children. That bond will exist between you forever, no matter how you choose to use it. You can be friendly, neutral, or hostile. But it is in your best interests, and those of your children, to use that bond in a positive way—with civility, decency, and a commitment to make the best of a difficult situation, for your children's sake, and your own.

. . . .

3

How to Manage Schedules, Clothes, Toys, School, and Money

I don't like the schedule. I hate going back and forth.
You know why? We don't have a Nintendo at my mom's
house. It's boring there. [Kim, age six.]

How do you decide on a schedule? Do you have to live near
your ex-spouse to have a successful joint-custody arrangement?
What about the clothes and the toys? More importantly, if you're
not used to making dinner for your kids and helping them with
their homework, how do you begin? What if your child gets sick?
And what about birthdays, holidays, and other vacations? This all
used to be so simple—nothing really to arrange. And the money,
oh the money! How will you ever figure out what's fair?

For most families in the midst of a divorce, the schedule is
what gets them through the night. There is comfort for everyone,

especially the children, in knowing where they will sleep and with which parent they will be. The schedule provides order in the midst of chaos and gives meaning to lives that seem to be falling apart.

The schedule can also be frightening to contemplate. It's very disconcerting for a mother who is used to having her children with her all the time to realize that she will be alone for the next four days. What will she do with herself? What meaning does her life have without the children? Conversely, a father who doesn't quite know how to entertain a five-year-old for three days in a row can be equally upset when the schedule goes into effect.

Setting Up a Schedule

When a couple plans to separate, they usually have some idea of what scheduling arrangements they want for their children. Sometimes these ideas are vague: Mother may feel that to be a good mother she has to allow her children equal access to their father, while Father may only know that he doesn't want to lose his children and that he wants to see them on a regular basis. Sometimes, neither parent really wants responsibility for the children, but they won't admit it. Not infrequently, parents disagree about custody and a full-scale custody battle erupts. More often than not, however, couples set a schedule that they hope will work in practice and won't disrupt the children's lives too much.

Suppose that you and your spouse are about to separate. You each want to maintain a close relationship with your children, so you decide on joint custody. Neither parent wants to let go, and neither parent wants to be without the children for long periods of time. It can be very helpful at a time like this to get some outside advice. Counselors, family therapists, mediators, and some lawyers are very skilled at helping you sort out the issues. The person you choose to talk with may not even be a professional but a friend or relative you trust who is willing to listen to your concerns. If you and your spouse know that you want to work out a joint-custody arrangement, find someone who will support your ideas about sharing responsibility for your children.

It's important to have a definite schedule before you separate, even though it may change. Your children need to have a clear idea of when they will see you again, and both parents need that security, too. No matter how young your children are, they need to know what is happening and where they will sleep on which nights. A two-year-old will not grasp the full meaning of your separation and its consequences, but should be told in much the same way that you would tell an older child. Explain the schedule, post a copy of it on the refrigerator, and go over it from time to time so that your children know what to expect. The clearer you can be about schedules, the easier it will be for your children to understand that their relationship with both parents will continue.

If you and your ex-spouse can set your angry feelings aside and be together in the same room, it is better to talk to your children together about the co-parenting plan. Children will sense that there is some cooperation between parents and that they can remain loving, involved people in their lives. It is a very frightening time for everyone. You can assure your children that it will take some time for all of you to adjust to new living arrangements. Your children will be best off in this difficult situation if you and your ex-partner are in touch with each other frequently and continue to plan together to meet your children's needs. If you plan to operate in this manner, tell your child.

If you don't think you will be able to be cooperative parents, it's time to rethink your plan so that the future is not difficult for your children. It's not a good idea for children to go back and forth between two homes where the atmosphere is hostile, with continual fighting between parents. Children in this situation are never free of tension and carry it with them from one home to the other.

Sample Schedules

When the Gordons separated, they developed a schedule for their children that they follow to this day, 11 years later. The children are with their mother from Wednesday after school until Sunday noon. They are with their dad from Sunday noon until Wednesday morning.

	MON.	TUES.	WED.	THUR.	FRI.	SAT.	SUN.
EVERY WEEK	X	X	X/Y	Y	Y	Y	Y/X

X represents days spent at the father's home
Y represents days spent at the mother's home

There is some flexibility in terms of holidays, vacations, and special occasions, but for the most part, the Gordons adhere to the schedule. Even after their oldest child went off to college and returned home on breaks, she adhered to the schedule. It was only in her sophomore year at college that she would spend her vacations sleeping at her mother's house. But she still had dinner at Dad's on his regular nights. Some people might feel this was a fairly rigid approach to joint custody, but for the Gordons it has worked out well. Although the parents decided on the schedule without consulting the children, the structure seemed to be a good support for everyone.

The Brewers have a different schedule, one that has evolved over the years. Their initial arrangement was based on a two-week time period:

	MON.	TUES.	WED.	THUR.	FRI.	SAT.	SUN.
WEEK I	Y	Y	X	X	X	X	X
WEEK II	Y	Y	X	X	Y	Y	Y
WEEK III	Y	Y	X	X	X	X	X
WEEK IV	Y	Y	X	X	Y	Y	Y

X represents days spent at the father's home
Y represents days spent at the mother's home

In this arrangement, the children always spent Mondays and Tuesdays with their mother, and Wednesdays and Thursdays with their father. The Friday, Saturday, Sunday period alternated every week. Each parent had a full child-free weekend and a long stretch of time to be with their children every two weeks.

With three children moving back and forth between two homes, however, this schedule became unwieldy. The Brewers' oldest son, Greg, began complaining about his friends not knowing where he was. Another child complained about moving his hockey gear back and forth. He frequently ended up at hockey practice without an essential piece of equipment. Their youngest child hadn't started to complain yet, but the Brewers knew it was just a matter of time.

The new schedule, adopted three years after their original plan, is based on a four-week period: two weeks spent with the father and then two weeks with the mother. The weekend in the middle of each two-week period, however, is spent with the other parent:

	MON.	TUES.	WED.	THUR.	FRI.	SAT.	SUN.
WEEK I	Y	Y	Y	Y	Y	X	X
WEEK II	Y	Y	Y	Y	Y	Y	Y
WEEK III	X	X	X	X	X	Y	Y
WEEK IV	X	X	X	X	X	X	X

X represents days spent at the father's home
Y represents days spent at the mother's home

This two-week schedule is particularly good for the Brewers, who want to limit the amount of time they have to spend talking to each other. If anything crucial comes up, they will speak to each other during the week. Otherwise, they talk only when the children are switching homes after two weeks, and then it is a very brief discussion about the children.

Other schedules include:

(1) Weekly—one week at the mother's house, then one week at the father's house.

(2) Semi-annual—six-month periods, with the child living with one parent for six months and then the other parent for the following six months.

(3) Annual—I have known several families in which the children lived on the West Coast for one year and then moved back to the East Coast the following year. One boy I know alternated living in Ireland for a year and then in the United States for the next year. He had been doing this for six years, changing schools, cultures, friends, and routines. Subsequently, his parents decided that he would stay in the United States for his four high-school years.

(4) Permanent—a situation in which the children never leave their home. For six months of each year, the mother lives in an apartment that her ex-husband vacates, and he moves into the family home. These parents don't want to disrupt their children's lives in any way and choose instead to be the ones to move back and forth. They visit regularly with their children when they are not the parent with primary responsibility.

Suzanne and Harvey have worked out an unusual arrangement for their three children. They each have separate apartments which they share with roommates. They then rotate two weeks in and two weeks out of the family home, which their children never leave. They chose this arrangement because they felt it would provide the most stability for the children. It may do that, but it also has created problems for the parents. Suzanne, a freelance artist, feels like a nomad: "I don't unpack my minivan. I'm on safari all the time—carrying around all the odd sorts of things I need to do my work." Harvey doesn't like tripping over his wife's clutter when he's in the family home: "I never liked it when we were married and I like it a lot less now. I spend my first few days back at the house cleaning up after her so I can live there in relative order."

The possibilities for creating a schedule, as well as the potential difficulties, are endless. To figure out what would make sense for you, consider the ages of your children, your children's

· · · · · · · · · ·

wishes (if they are older), your work schedule, and other time commitments and geographical factors. Parents often experiment with a variety of schedules before finding one that works well for everyone. What may work well at one stage of your postdivorce life may be inappropriate several years later.

Changing the Schedule

We separated when Nicole was two years old. I wasn't confident in myself as a mother, and I was pleased that her father and I could work out a 50–50 co-parenting agreement. He already had a girl friend and they seemed to be a stable couple, and I was grateful for that. I thought Nicole could benefit from this arrangement. We split the week in half and we followed this schedule for four years, until Nicole was six. At that time, Alexander and Sloane, now his wife, went to Australia for six months. At first, I was very upset and didn't think I could handle Nicole on my own. It turned out to be the best time for us. I taught her how to read, how to ride a bike. Everything my father had taught me how to do, I taught Nicole. I felt competent for the first time in my life. [Sandra]

When Nicole was six, her parents switched to a weekly schedule: one week at Mom's, one week at Dad's. They had always lived in the same community and so geography was not a problem. The problem arose when Nicole was nine. Even though there were toys and clothes at each house, Nicole would always pack a suitcase full of her favorite things and cart them back and forth each week.

"She started feeling that she was living out of a suitcase and then that she *was* the suitcase," says Alexander. "Her mother and I agreed that it would be best for Nicole to live with her mother on a full-time basis, and that she would be with me one night during the week and every other weekend." Nicole, now 13, was very pleased with her new schedule.

What worked when Nicole was two years old no longer was

suitable at age nine. Her parents lived near one another, and she shared her time between them for seven years. Although she no longer lives with her father and his wife, Nicole is extremely loyal to them and feels a closeness to her father that she doesn't think she would have, had she lived with just her mother during her early years.

It took Julia and George four years to create a schedule they could live with. Initially, George moved out and left Rachel and Randy to live with their mother. He would come and stay with the children on weekends, when Julia would move out and stay with friends. The following year, George returned to the house, and Julia lived with a group of friends. Three days a week, Julia would be in the house, and George would leave. Not surprisingly, this plan became difficult for both Julia and George, and for a number of reasons, they both returned to the house.

"This was an extremely stressful time for all of us," says Julia. "We lived in separate bedrooms until we negotiated a new agreement, and we had to go to a counselor to do it."

The new agreement stipulated that Julia would get her own apartment, which George would help her finance. The children would then move back and forth between the house, which George would keep, and Julia's apartment. Time is now divided equally between the parents. "I suppose it didn't have to take us four years to work it out, but we didn't know any other way to do it," says George.

Some parents have not been able to agree upon a schedule and instead have one imposed on them by the court. The Browns have been transferring four children back and forth between homes *every day.* The children go to their mother's house after school until 7:30 p.m. Their father picks them up there every night. They sleep at his house and catch the school bus the next morning. Weekends are alternated.

This schedule is actually an improvement over the one they had when I first saw them in my office. Previously, the children woke up at 6 a.m.; Dad drove them to Mom's and she drove them

. . . .

to school and picked them up at 3 p.m. Mom had the children until 6 p.m., when Dad would come and get them. The children complained to me about having to get up so early in the morning. Neither parent wanted to give up any time with the children, and another court battle loomed. These children had already been tested by psychologists, evaluated by a court-appointed psychiatrist, talked to by lawyers, and in every way torn asunder. The court ordered counseling.

Enough was enough. I told the Browns that their ongoing animosity was destroying their children. It was time to put an end to the warfare. Reports from the school guidance counselor indicated that the children were having serious problems. The antagonism that these parents felt toward each other was putting tremendous pressure on their children, and their effectiveness as parents was severely limited. The children were being used in an endless tug-of-war, and the battle left scars on every family member.

Counseling enabled these parents to work out some differences in a neutral setting—in this case, my office. They made changes to the schedule without going back to court, they discussed the need to spend some time with each child separately, and they worked out a plan to provide some continuity in helping the children with their homework.

While this schedule may seem extremely unwieldy, it does take into account the parents' work schedule. Mom now works from 8 a.m. to 3 p.m. and is available to the children after school. Dad has arranged his time so that he is at the office from 9 a.m. (giving him time to get the children up, dressed, fed, and off to school) to 6 p.m. "This gives me time to collect myself and stop off at the supermarket before I go collect the children," says the father. "And we don't have to pay for child care. One of us is always available to the children."

Private Time

How many children do you have? Do you want all of your children to be with you at the same time? Or do you want some time when you can be alone with one child?

Some parents feel very strongly that their children should have the continuity of sibling relationships, especially at a time when the family itself is not stable. They also see the importance of spending some time alone with each child, so they work that into their schedule.

"We call it private time," says Lois. "Our schedule is that the children spend two weeks with their father and two weeks with me. On the transition weekend, Michael makes the switch on Friday night and Rebecca stays with me until Sunday night. That way we each get to spend one weekend a month with one child." Other parents feel that their children have individual needs and that split custody makes more sense.

When John got to be 15, I can practically remember the day, he told me he was not changing homes any more. And so he doesn't. He lives with me full time and his younger brother still follows the regular, 50–50 schedule. I wonder if and when he'll make the same announcement. That would be fine with me but I know it would be hard on their mother. [Stan]

It *would* be very hard on Lisa, their mother. She already feels terrible about giving up her oldest son, and the prospect of living without her youngest son is not pleasant. "Maybe if we didn't have joint custody all along it would never have come to this," says Lisa. "I don't know. I do know I hate being without both my boys."

The only positive thing for Lisa is that she feels she truly has quality time with both her children. She and her older son have dinner dates—very special times for them both. When Lisa and her "baby" are together, it is just the two of them, there's no

. . . .

sibling rivalry to deal with, and Lisa can devote herself to her younger son. "If I don't look at the positives in this crazy situation, I would really go nuts," says Lisa.

Some parents do not set aside specific time to be with each child, but find that there is time to be with them separately. Julia says, "It just works out that Randy gets home from school quite a bit before Rachel does, so we have that time alone. And then Randy goes to bed before Rachel does, so she and I have quiet time together in the evening. I do get to be with them as individual children and we all like that a lot."

Toys and Clothes

In many joint-custody families, the issue of how to manage clothes and toys at each house is an annoyance, but one that is easily handled. Of course, if parents are fighting, every toy bought at one house but left at the other can be a reason for a flare-up. Parents usually realize, though, that as much as they might plan to have two sets of clothing and toys at each house, something might go wrong. A child who realizes that a favorite toy is at the other house can become very upset. Many parents, feeling guilty that their children have to live this way, make every effort to get the toy. Lee, a father of two young boys, says: "My philosophy has been to drop whatever I'm doing and drive whatever they want to the other house as soon as possible. It's not their fault they have to live like this, so I do what I can to compensate."

Lois agrees:

Our agreement is that if the children leave something at my apartment and want it at their father's, it's my responsibility to get it there. The same holds true for him. If they leave something at their father's apartment and find they want it when they get to my place, he has to get it here. This has cut down considerably on things being left behind inadvertently. Before they leave, I ask if they've got everything they're going to need for the next two weeks.

I know I don't want to be making extra trips across town to bring them a book report or a pair of sneakers.

Ask your children which toys they'd like to have at each house. This is important to most children. A four-year-old associates certain toys with one parent or the other. Children know which parent likes to play board games and which is good at jigsaw puzzles. It would be overwhelming for a young child to be completely responsible for dividing the toys, but you can help your child make some decisions about which toys go where. And then don't blame your child or argue with your ex-spouse if the toys end up somewhere else. Tommy, age 11, says that if he brings a toy over to his mother's house to use for the weekend, she says he has to leave it there. "It's very confusing to me, but there's nothing much I can do about it," he says.

As children get older, you can expect them to take more responsibility for knowing where their possessions are. Yes, you are asking a lot of your children, but you need to help them adjust to this part of their life. A ten-year-old boy can be helped to gather up his things the night before he switches homes and asked to think about what he needs for the days ahead.

"I have to remember to ask whose weekend is coming up and if we're doing anything special," says Tommy. "I have to know what to bring over. I want to be prepared." Most children are able to manage this level of responsibility with some help, although some definitely cannot. (For more information about the effects of joint-custody living on children, see Chapter 4.)

Do children need a set of clothes at each house? No, but it helps.

My brother and I have to pack up these big suitcases and walk over to the other house. People think we're running away from home and it gets embarrassing because we have to go right past the bus stop. [Kathy, age 13]

Jim and Charlotte each took responsibility for buying clothes for their daughter, Julie, at their separate apartments. "I know some couples who got into fighting about what dress got left where," says Charlotte. "We've always been very respectful of each other about that. If it ended up that some things which Jim bought Julie were at my house, at the end of the month I'd make up a bag and send that back over." Julie, now 17, does her own clothes shopping and is completely in charge of what clothes are at which house.

In order to be sure that her daughters would have nice things at their father's house, Naomi bought them sheets and towels as well as clothes. Naomi has always been responsible for their clothes at both houses, and Mark for their medical care. Dividing the responsibility in that way has eliminated a potential source of conflict for them.

Choosing a Place to Call Home

Some children, especially older ones, express preferences for living arrangements. They don't like changing homes, even if they have possessions in both places. They want their friends to be able to call them at one house, they want to decorate and clean up one room only.

One boy I know lived in a co-parenting situation from the time he was five years old until he was 12. Then, his father and his father's new wife decided to move to another state. The boy, Chris, wanted to go with them. It was an extremely difficult situation for his mother, Lynn. She felt great pain and loss at the realization that she would not have a daily relationship with her son. Yet she also wanted to respect her son's decision and agreed to his move.

I had a similar experience when my son, Josh, at age 14, moved with his father to Burlington, Vermont. Jeff and I had agreed when we separated that whoever left Philadelphia, left without Josh. Yet that agreement didn't seem to matter much when Josh said he wanted to be with his dad. I didn't feel I could hold

him here against his will, yet I knew how sad I would be to see
Josh go. The story of his move and how we handled it is recounted
in my book, *Long Distance Parenting: A Guide for Divorced
Parents*. In that book, other parents and children also relate the
heartache of being apart and the commitment they have to
overcome geographic obstacles and deepen their relationships.

I am often asked if I think our joint-custody arrangement of
ten years was a failure, since Jeff chose to move and discontinue
the arrangement. I do not think our parenting agreement was a
failure. Rather, it set the stage for Josh to have meaningful
relationships with both his parents, one he lived with and one who
was 400 miles away. Jeff and I were able to continue our
partnership in parenting that we started so many years ago, co-
parenting now across the miles. If you have joint custody and have
been successful in sharing the responsibilities of parenting, and it
now appears that your ex-spouse is planning to move, I strongly
suggest that you and your ex-spouse consider how you can
continue to provide your child with ongoing, close relationships
with both parents. Your child's well-being requires an extra degree
of cooperation and communication between parents, so that the
upheaval in your lives can be withstood as best as possible.

Jan told the following story of her son's decision to live with
his father:

*When Stefan started complaining that he felt like a yo-yo, moving
back and forth from week to week, we switched to a month-by-
month schedule. We each wanted that continuity, going through
school days and weekends. At the end of the month it was like a
huge caravan that would move from one house to the other. Then
Stefan said he still felt like a yo-yo and he hated it when he had to
leave one house and go to the other. This spring, at the wise old
age of ten, Stefan told me, "You know, Mom, when I was littler, I
needed you. You were my mommy. And I didn't know Daddy very
well.' He said, "Well, I'm ten now and I'm a boy and I want to
grow up to be a man like my father. I don't want this to hurt*

. . . .

your feelings, but can I live with my father? I need to stay in one place."

It did hurt my feelings, but I was really glad that he could say this to me and told him we would work it out. He really needed one neighborhood and one room. Stefan bicycles over to see me every afternoon, so it isn't like a real separation.

What would you have done in Jan's situation? Some parents would argue that even a ten-year-old is too young to make that decision and that Jan should have insisted that they continue the month-by-month schedule. Did Stefan's father coach him on what to say? His words sound like something a father in his position might suggest. There are no rules about listening and responding to a child's wishes. You need to know your child. By asking to live with one parent, a child may be asking for more time with that other parent. Or he may, in fact, be saying that switching homes every week is just too much to manage. Whatever the stated reasons for a request to change the schedule, it's important to pay attention and try to understand the underlying reasons for the request.

It's not a good idea to ask young children about their preferences for living arrangements. To do so would create undue strain on a child who is not equipped to make such a decision. Some parents do ask their young children where they want to live. Answers are often determined by which house has what kind of toys. On what other basis could a six-year-old make such a choice? No child wants to choose one parent over the other. Loyalty is important to children of divorce. To ask a child to choose a parent will make a child feel terribly disloyal. One parent will feel hurt and betrayed, and the child could lose the love of that parent. It's the responsibility of the parents to make this decision for their young children.

Some parents do not give their children a voice in the matter even as they get older. "We never wanted the children to have to choose between us," says Mark. "Naomi and I never asked them, they never complained, and so the schedule has stayed the same for 11 years."

. . . .

Marla Isaacs, Ph.D., co-author of *The Difficult Divorce*, says that many children who have lived in joint-custody arrangements for a long time don't dare say, "Enough!" "They are so into things being equal, almost to the point of counting hours," says Dr. Isaacs, "that to request a change in scheduling represents a taboo."

Lois and Marvin wrote into their separation agreement that they would negotiate the schedule every year. Says Lois:

Part of that negotiation process involves surveying what our two children want. Both Marvin and I feel it's very important to keep listening to the children, to hear their needs. They're getting older now, we know their needs will change, and we want to be open to meeting their needs. So that's why we wrote it in our agreement. And we read that part of the agreement to the children, so that they'd know we were very serious about listening to them.

Is it only boys who choose to live with their fathers? What about girls? Do they always stay with their mothers? Adolescents often choose to live with the parent of the same sex. Teenage girls often ask to live full time with their mothers, even after many years of 50–50 living in two homes, unless their relationships with their mothers are turbulent. However, circumstances can change this pattern. For example, when a mother moves away with a new husband, her daughter may prefer to stay in familiar surroundings, with her father. Even when parents remain in the same community, it is not unusual for the schedule to change as the child gets older.

Julie, now 17, has been living in two homes since she was three years old:

First we split the week, then we alternated weeks, then we alternated two weeks. Now I live with my mom for three weeks and my dad for one week. I see my dad on Wednesdays during the weeks when I'm at my mom's house and I spend a lot of time with my dad during the summer. I guess you could say we've done it all. The big change is that now I can drive, so I can see either parent whenever I want to, and no one has to drive me over.

Many couples have seen that a schedule that worked well when they first separated was no longer desirable when their children were five or ten years older. Contemplating changes in routine may be anxiety-producing, but it's important to be realistic: things do change.

Along with changes in the children's needs and wishes, your own work schedule may change. You may have more night meetings, or new responsibilities that encroach on weekends. Some parents choose to keep the same schedule and find babysitters when they are not available to be with the children. Others will talk to each other and attempt to work out a better schedule so that the children are with one of them at all times, or at least as much as possible.

Should you and your ex-spouse live close to each other? When Mark bought the house next door to his former home with Naomi, Naomi was uncomfortable, and friends thought it was strange. Were Mark and Naomi divorced, or not? Each of them had already remarried, yet some felt that living so close to each other would be detrimental.

I was mortified when I first heard that Mark was buying the home next to mine. I thought it was much too close. It has worked out well, though, being neighbors and friends. It's easy for me to see my children, even when it's their dad's day. We're there for each other in emergencies, we take care of each others' families, and it's understood we'll go out of our way for each other. [Naomi]

Mark's second wife, Heather, had this to say:

Most people react to how close we live. I find it's the least significant issue. Feelings are powerful, and that's what you have to deal with no matter where you live. Transition time has been more difficult for Mark's children because they're out of one home and in the next in a matter of minutes. Overall, though, it's been extremely convenient.

It may not be convenient for you to see your ex-spouse in the supermarket. You may not feel comfortable with the idea that you might run into your ex-spouse and his lover at your friendly neighborhood movie theater. The local shopkeepers assume you are still married, since you both still frequent the same stores, and the pharmacist may not understand why you need two bottles of cough medicine instead of one. Knowing that your ex-spouse lives nearby can be a positive or a negative experience for you, or both. On the one hand, there's the comfort of knowing that you can get help in an emergency; but the process of separating emotionally may be more difficult when you still live practically within earshot of your former spouse.

What living arrangements would best suit your own needs? Perhaps the neighborhood where you've been living as an intact family is not suited for single parenthood. Suburban life may seem stifling now that you've separated, and as much as you want to be close to your children, you feel that living in your old neighborhood would be very unsatisfying to you. There are several alternatives to consider.

One plan would be to stay in the same locale for a year or so while you and your children adjust to a new way of living. You would be able to maintain close contact with your children, and you could spend some of your child-free time discovering other parts of the city that appeal to you, for future reference. If you decide to remain in the same area for now, that doesn't mean forever. For now, you have chosen to live close to your ex-spouse in order to work out an easier system of joint custody.

Or you might decide to move away from your neighborhood. You may have to do some extra driving to get your children to school and to arrange visits with friends. If your children form friendships in your new locale, these visits will probably become less necessary over time, although school friends are usually the most important.

The Brewers decided to live about three miles apart, but still in the same school district. The distance was important to them; they didn't want to run into each other everywhere they went. They also didn't want to make life more difficult for their children by asking them to live far from their friends. The children can bike to their friends' houses, and, when necessary, driving them isn't a problem. Their oldest child can drive and enjoys the role of chauffeur for the younger children.

The Amatos live half an hour away from each other, in different school districts. This has caused innumerable problems for all of them. The court order requires that the two children go to school from their mother's house. Father has to drive them to and from school on his days. That has become manageable. But where do the children play after-school sports? Which parent will drive Matt to soccer practice and Judd to tennis practice? One parent will have to make an extra effort on some days to be sure that there is continuity for the children. If the Amatos were on good terms, this would be less of an issue. Since their relationship is a hostile one, however, every sports event becomes an occasion for tension.

Not only is the practice before a game a potential time for conflict, so is the game itself. Will both parents show up? Can they sit on the same side of the field without glaring at one another? As Jack describes it, the situation worsens if one of the children gets a trophy:

If the children get an award, or a plaque, or a trophy on Jacqueline's day, she wants the award to be kept in her house. Never mind that I paid for their sports activities, all their equipment, and went to every game. I tell the children that the trophy or plaque is theirs. I'm not battling over a piece of wood.

For the Amato children, joint custody has meant being witness to ongoing hostilities between their parents. Yes, the children have a schedule. Yes, they have toys and clothes at both houses. But it is not the logistics that set the tone for their lives. Rather, it is the discord and animosity that they carry with them from one house to the other.

School Schedules

One area where confusion seems to be the norm rather than the exception is school. If a school has little familiarity with joint custody, it may become problematic for the school to list two addresses and phone numbers in the school directory, for its computer to send out two sets of notices for one child, and for some teachers and administrators to relate to two involved parents living in two separate homes. Naomi remembers:

We were the only joint-custody family in town, so when I called the school to ask them to send out two sets of every notice and to list both Mark and myself in the school directory, they said they'd do it, but they never did. I was vigilant in keeping Mark informed, but he always felt like the lesser parent.

Naomi would call Mark about every school event, but she resented reminding him. It felt too similar to an aspect of their marriage that was unpleasant for both of them. As a result of their pressure on the school, and an increase in the number of joint-custody families, school policy has changed so that both parents' names and addresses are listed in the school directory.

Sally and Vic report that many things have slipped through the cracks because they don't both get notices from school and because they are not in close communication with one another. They, too, have asked the school to let them each know about important events and to send each parent a copy of report cards. Sally missed an important parent/teacher meeting and Vic remembers missing a play their daughter was in. These missed opportunities remain a sore spot for both of them. Some teachers, Sally recalls, have a special interest in their child and take it upon themselves to see that important messages get to both parents. Sally and Vic are most appreciative of those efforts, but they are the exception, not the rule.

Evan, age ten, is in a joint-custody family, but his parents are continually battling. He always gets two notices from school, but his mom often takes both notices so his dad won't know about events and then won't show up.

"I hide the notices from her if I can so I can show it to Dad and he will know about things, too," says Evan. The school is doing its part, but in this case, the parents are thwarting efforts at total participation and involvement by the other.

Whether you go to school conferences together depends on your own feelings. Some parents are able to use that time constructively, to evaluate their child's performance in school, while others feel so tense being in the same room with their ex-spouse that they can barely hear what the teacher is saying. Most teachers will accommodate a request to schedule two separate conferences if necessary. There is usually only one "Open School" night, however, and one six-year-old I know whose parents recently separated took the opportunity to leave them a note in her desk. It read: "Dear Mommy and Daddy, I love you both very much and it's been very hard for me since I've been living in two homes. Love, Hilary."

It can be a frustrating, time-consuming task to educate teachers and school administrators about what it means to have two divorced parents who are both still intimately involved in the lives of their children. Considering the importance of education and the amount of time your child will spend in school, your communication and patience with school personnel is important to the success of your joint-custody plan.

When the Schedule Varies

Other potential sources of conflict involve illness, birthdays, vacations, and holidays—anything that can cause the schedule to vary. One of the most memorable moments when I appeared on "The Phil Donahue Show" came when I said that when my son got sick and was at my house, I didn't automatically assume that I had to care for him. I'd call my ex-husband and we'd see which one of us had the lighter work responsibilities that day, and then we'd decide who could take care of our son. Members of the audience were appalled, and they let me know it by booing and hissing. How selfish could I be? Fathers didn't know how to take care of sick children anyway, they said. But for Josh, this system meant that he would be cared for by the parent best able to give him the attention he needed.

Vacations

Vacations need to be scheduled in advance as much as possible. If you know that you want to take the children for a two-week trip in six months, tell your ex-spouse now. If you want to go somewhere by yourself, confirm these plans with your ex-spouse to see if she can be with the children then. This is one area in which most couples can accommodate each other. Not so with the Amatos, however. Their court order stipulates that they each have two weeks vacation a year with the children and that they have to notify each other in writing 30 days prior to vacation time. Once, Jack thought that he was complying with the court order and went out of his way to accommodate his ex-wife when she changed her plans at the last moment, only to find that she refused to let the children be with him during the Christmas holiday that he had planned. His error was that he had communicated a change in plans through the children, not in writing. Jacqueline threatened to call the police if the children were not back at her house at the usual time. Jack didn't want to risk causing a scene and disturbing his children's Christmas holiday even more, so he returned the children as usual and spent the week by himself.

Many families alternate major holidays such as Thanksgiving and Christmas on a yearly basis. Others agree to divide the important days in half, so that each parent gets to be with the children. Some families plan to divide an important meal in two—dinner here, desserts there. Still others decide to keep to the schedule, no matter what. Some families are able to celebrate holidays together.

The Gordons enjoy getting together for special events, such as children's birthdays, with all the members of both families: Naomi and her second husband, Dave, and their son; Mark and his second wife, Heather, and her two children; and Naomi and Mark's two children. Together they have celebrated many occasions. Naomi and Mark feel a spirit of camaraderie and pride in their expanded family unit and in being successful at maintaining friendly relationships after divorce.

Parents like the Gordons established a schedule that they still keep, 11 years later. Other families, like the Brewers, have changed their schedule several times over the years. When a schedule is court-ordered, as it is for the Amato family, the parents go back to court for a revision. For any family, a schedule provides structure during a time that is anything but ordered. In the wise words of Tommy, age 11, "It's easy to follow if you know what you're doing."

Money

I get $30 a week for the three weeks a month Julie lives with me. In the summer, I pay Jim that amount for the weeks she's there. When I get my $90 checks, I try not to spend the money all in one place. [Charlotte]

Money, and fighting over it, embitters people. Charlotte is very resentful, as you can see. She knows that Jim has more money than she does, yet he makes things difficult for her, and, by implication, for their daughter as well. Would she go to court to get more money from Jim? "Never!" she says emphatically. "I'd probably end up paying a lawyer more money than I'd ever get from Jim." Using the court system has never appealed to Charlotte's sense of fairness and sharing in the costs of raising their child.

Charlotte is not alone in her economic struggle and in her aversion to using an adversarial system to solve her problems. Many women, earning far less than their former husbands, are faced with the problem of reconciling their desire to share the costs of raising their children, their pride in wanting to do so, and their lowered earning power. Charlotte and Jim are in the same profession, yet he earns considerably more money. Jim has some family money; Charlotte does not. Each has a long-term relationship with someone else now, although they keep their finances separate.

Other parents I have interviewed didn't want to be bothered by working out financial arrangements and thought that if they did, their fairly amicable relationship would be threatened.

"I never pressured Steve about money," says Molly. "I didn't want to make things difficult by causing a ruckus."

When Molly and Steve separated, they agreed that Steve would continue to pay the mortgage (the house is still in both their names) and would pay no child support, even though Molly, a high-school graduate, had just started to work after years of being at home. If an expense came up that was too difficult for Molly to handle alone, she'd talk to Steve and present it as a one-time thing: "If Steve was in a good mood, he'd come through."

In order to keep the peace, Molly asked very little of Steve. Instead, her boyfriend started to buy things for her son Owen, such as a bike. "Money has always been a major source of irritation," says Molly. "I never thought Steve was generous to me and he always thought he was going way overboard."

Molly is one of those women whose standard of living was

lowered by divorce. Now, years later, she earns about one-third of what her ex-husband earns. The mortgage payment remains the same. There was no provision for child support, although Steve always considered that he was giving Molly more than the court would have required.

In her book *Mothers on Trial*, Phyllis Chesler says she feels that mothers become impoverished in joint-custody situations when they make financial agreements because they are fearful of losing custody or becoming embroiled in a custody battle. Molly never wanted to be involved in the court system; she always felt one-down and was afraid if she took Steve to court for child support, he might sue for custody and she would lose her child. Besides, she could never have afforded a lawyer.

Paula Rosen, Ph.D., a family therapist specializing in issues of divorce and custody, offers this advice: "Be very generous and very fair. If there's anything that will ruin a postdivorce relationship, money will." She has seen many mothers become impoverished by financial settlements, fathers who have taken out their anger on their ex-wives by withholding financial support, and children who feel embittered as the years go on.

It's not unusual for college students to be caught in the middle. "Tell your father to reimburse me for his share of the plane ticket," they are told, or "Tell your mother to pay her share of the tuition." Dr. Rosen feels it is the responsibility of parents to handle their financial obligations to their children. Anything less creates acrimony and heartache.

When figuring out finances, there's always the initial shock of realizing that the same amount of money that took care of one household now must take care of two. Is there a way to decrease expenses, or somehow increase income? Patricia Bogin Wisch, Ed.D., a psychologist and Director of Mediation Services of Philadelphia, thinks that it's reasonable for a divorcing woman to expect to live the same lifestyle—for a time. "A contract was made years ago, and the results are that she will never be able to earn his income. She should be compensated for that." Dr. Wisch does suggest that divorced mothers go back to school and begin working outside the home, if they haven't been doing so already. The economics of the 1990s are that two incomes are usually needed to support even one household, and especially two.

Sandra and Alexander have never exchanged money for their daughter, Nicole, no matter what the schedule has been. "I never asked for child support or for alimony," says Sandra. "I didn't want it. I've been real independent of him. I've led my life the way I wanted. No regrets, no resentments." Occasionally, Alexander has bought clothes. He paid for braces when Sandra asked, and he will pay for college expenses. "We have an unusual relationship," says Sandra. "When my business went under, Alexander gave me $5,000. It was much cheaper than child support would have been, although he didn't have to do that. I appreciated it a lot."

Many of the joint-custody families I have interviewed either split costs 50–50, or divide them based on their income and ability to pay. Some parents do this systematically, look at each other's income tax returns, and leave nothing to chance. Others go on the honor system.

"Naomi and I have always acted in good faith," says Mark. "I earn much more than she does, and I never wanted to make things difficult for her and the children." When they separated, Mark and Naomi estimated their separate incomes and agreed to child support for Naomi based on a percentage of their incomes.

"I got the house, which was a good thing," says Naomi, "because I never would have been able to afford buying another one if we sold it and split the proceeds." They agreed to a cost-of-living increase that has never been instituted. When Naomi remarried, Mark's share of child support was lowered.

"The agreement states that I get both kids as a tax deduction," says Naomi, "and I have always given Mark one. The agreement says he pays for all summer expenses, but we've always split that. I've gone out of my way to be fair and I know Mark has, too." Mark agrees: "If either of us felt ripped off by the other, we could never be as friendly as we are," he says. This divorced couple, on friendly terms, manage their finances the way they manage their relationship—openly, fairly, and with a spirit of cooperation.

The Brewers split the costs of raising their three children 50–50. They keep track of expenses and reconcile accounts every few months. This does not include routine expenses that they assume are equal (since they have a 50–50 custody arrangement), such as food, entertainment, birthday presents for other kids, and school supplies. "The most difficult thing about this," says Vic, "is that I have to maintain contact with my ex-wife. For all her wonderful qualities, I would be just as happy to see her maybe once every other year."

Tony Brown was ordered to pay $600 a month support for his four children. This was meant to equalize the pay differential between him and his ex-wife. From this amount, Arlene was to pay for child care during the day, all meals, and half of the support for the children. In theory, medical bills, clothing, and school supplies were to be split 50–50; Arlene was to pay for lunches at school; and Tony would keep the family home, since the children sleep at his house every night, except for every other weekend.

But here is Tony's chart of how expenses *actually* tabulated:

Expenses	*Court (theory)*	*Actual*
medical	50/50	father 100%
clothing	50/50	father 99%
school supplies	50/50	father 100%
lunches at school	mother 100%	father 100%
house to live in	father 100%	father 100%

Yes, Tony thinks this is unfair. No, he's not going back to court, even though he knows his ex-wife's salary has increased.

. . . .

Nor is he interested in being petty. "I have so much to do just taking care of the kids, the house, and myself," says Tony, "that I have no time for nickels and dimes." For him, it's easier to pay more than he agreed to than to fight it.

Arlene's job allows her to be home with the children after school and pays less than a full-time job. She feels that the amount of child support she receives is fair and takes into account her ability to be home in the afternoons.

How have you worked out your finances? Do you feel comfortable with your arrangement, or are there lingering feelings of resentment?

Money matters absorb a great deal of time and emotion after a divorce. It's difficult to establish what is fair, how to compensate for a woman's job of working inside the home and not having any income or credit rating of her own, how to figure out which expenses are the child's, and what might be considered the mother's. At best it is a complicated business. Being fair, being reasonable, and being generous in money matters goes a long way to ease the pain of a separation for everyone in the family.

In my clinical work, I have seen families spend more on legal fees than on child support. In these cases, less money is available for the children's care, and more acrimony is the result. I urge parents not to take out their anger on one another through finances.

When expenses are prorated according to income, there is usually a sense of fairness and cooperation between parents. "I'm a nurse but I stayed home after Erica was born," says Andrea. "Roger and I split expenses 80–20, but I'm sure my contribution will increase as Erica gets older and I work more. I want that to happen."

Here are some examples of how other joint-custody families have worked out their financial arrangements:

We have the same income, so we split monies evenly. We account for all our finances quarterly. If there was a bill that was more than $200, we pay that up right away. [Lois]

• • • • • • • • • •

71

Neither of us wanted to be bothered with personal finances. We pay proportionate to our incomes for school tuition and other large expenses. We both have a need not to pry. [Sol]

I get to claim Dana as a tax deduction. I pay all her major expenses—tuition, medical expenses, camp. I pay for most of her needs. I'm just more able to handle the finances. Dennis is a schoolteacher and doesn't make as much as I do. [Monica]

We're pretty easygoing about money, although sometimes I think my ex-wife is too frivolous with my money. The kids always have what they need and that's what's important to me. [Ken]

My ex-husband is irresponsible about money. He was during our marriage and he is now. If I allowed myself, I'd be very upset about this all the time. I just have to go on with my life. I have a good job, so I take care of everything financially. I've given up trying to get him to be any different. In the meantime, my kids are well taken care of. Bitter? Of course I am. Wouldn't you be?'' [Zoe]

I don't look at it as money, where one does this much and the other does that much. Whatever we have to do, we do. My income is much higher than Sheila's. We have a lot of trust between us now, so that she can call me up to say she needs some money. I don't feel benevolent about it either. It's just not important to me. There's a friendship and I'm doing it because she's a friend of mine, not because I feel obligated. We have a name for it: we call it friends who happen to be parents of the same children. [Charles]

Statistics show that the standard of living for women and children is reduced dramatically after a divorce, while the standard of living for men usually increases. While it is often difficult to determine what is fair, don't allow your family to become part of these statistics.

. . . .

Extend yourself if you earn more money than your ex-spouse, no matter what the reason is for your divorce. Your children did not ask for this and should not be caught in the middle of a financial war between their parents. If you earn the lesser amount of money, be fair and be willing to compromise. Use the services of a family mediator to help you settle your financial arrangements. If you are not satisfied with the arrangement you have now, work to change it. Don't let bitterness and resentment rule your life. Your children deserve better, and so do you.

4

....

Helping Your Child Adjust

*I like our 50–50 schedule because this way I get to
spend equal time with each parent and I don't get tired
or incredibly mad at one.* [Carrie, age 12]

*Basically, joint custody is depressing. It means your
parents are divorced and* that's *depressing.*
[Samantha, age 14]

*The structure is good for my parents. It keeps them from
arguing so much. I'm not so sure about whether it's
good for me.* [Bob, age 15]

There's no getting around it: divorce is extremely difficult for
children, regardless of custody arrangements. Children in joint-

custody situations, as well as those in sole-custody families, have a hard time adjusting to their new lives. Even when children appear relatively stable in the years immediately following divorce, long-lasting effects can appear when these children become young adults.

When their parents separate, children are upset. They feel angry, sad, depressed, and confused. Their lives are in a state of upheaval, regardless of what new living arrangements their parents create for them. Everything around them is changing, and the uncertainty of their world at this time causes them pain and distress.

Children show their pain in many ways. Some may develop sleeping problems, others may become withdrawn, and others may have trouble concentrating on their school work. The extent of these difficulties varies with individual children, their ages, and their home situations. A boy who has heard his parents fighting may feel relieved after their separation, once there is peace at home. But mostly he feels sad that his parents had to separate. He experiences a tremendous loss in his life—the loss of his family. One boy I know said, "It will never be the same again. There's been a death here. The whole family died."

On the other hand, a girl whose parents did not argue may be confused about why her parents had to separate, and may have trouble understanding why this disruption in her life was necessary. She doesn't understand the notion of people growing apart, or falling out of love. She worries about who will take care of her, and whether she will be able to see both her parents, and where she will live. Many children of divorce, especially younger ones, blame themselves for the divorce. Assurances by parents that "Mommy and Daddy still love you," "this is our divorce, not yours," and so on, bear repeating many times. Your words may have a hollow ring to a child who feels frightened, anxious, and very confused. What she does understand is that her world is falling apart.

Children carry the scars of the divorce process with them through the years. Not that the parents don't as well, but children

· · · · · · · · ·

are more vulnerable, less able to bounce back, and they experience divorce as the most significant, traumatic event of their lives. Important research is being done on the long-lasting effects of divorce on children. Judith S. Wallerstein, Ph.D., co-author with Sandra Blakeslee of *Second Chances* and co-author with Joan Berlin Kelly of *Surviving the Break-Up*, identifies the overburdened child as one who feels responsible for caring for one or both of his parents and, at the same time, feels less cared for himself. This is the child who becomes his parents' primary support system, friend, advisor—any number of roles. The child's needs don't get met. Rather, he tries, unsuccessfully, to see to it that his parents' needs are met.

Deborah's description of her relationship with her daughter fits this picture:

At times I've made mistakes, putting too much weight on my relationship with my daughter. She really is the most important person in my life and I worry sometimes about feeling too close to her. I don't know how other parents feel about their kids, but I do know that she is just about everything there is in the world to me. And I think that's unhealthy for a mother to love a child so much. I worry if I'm depending on her too much and treating her too much like my friend and not enough like my little girl.

Staying Involved with Your Child

The results of research by Wallerstein and others point to the difficulties that children of divorce experience a decade and more after a divorce takes place. Many young adults whose parents divorced when they were younger face problems forming their own intimate relationships, establishing careers, and forging their own identities. Some are apprehensive about getting married for fear their own marriages will dissolve. Others are terrified of commitment of any sort. The wounds are slow to heal, and the scars are often permanent.

. . . .

Given this dismal picture, is there anything, you might ask, that would alter these dire predictions? Only if their parents ". . . resumed their parenting roles, managed to put their differences aside, and allowed the children a continuing relationship with both parents," says Wallerstein, do children tend to do well after divorce. Unfortunately, it was the minority of children in her study who had these advantages.

What does allowing the children a continuing relationship with both parents really mean? Some people believe that it means equal access to both parents, while others feel that sole custody with liberal visitation rights fits this criteria. Perhaps joint legal custody would ensure a continuing relationship with both parents. Even if the time is not equally divided, parents who have joint physical custody might ensure a continuing relationship. Or, every other weekend with the other parent, with a midweek dinner every now and then, might suffice. It's hard to know what is best for your own child.

Many of these issues are confusing, but it is well established that divorce heightens a child's sense of abandonment. Every child of divorce loses a parent, usually the one who moves out. Even if that parent maintains a close relationship, the child still experiences the abandonment. The child also wonders: if one parent moved out, what will keep the other one home? Wallerstein and Blakeslee maintain that the main concern for young children in joint-custody and sole-custody arrangements remains the same: fear of abandonment.

Children bond with both parents. "Research using infants' protest at separation, greeting behavior on reunion, and comfort seeking when distressed have consistently shown that most children appear to be attached to both parents by eight months of age," says Robert E. Adler, Ph.D., author of *Sharing the Children*. Children look to both parents for reassurance. They need the bond with both their parents in order to develop all of who they are. Both mothers and fathers contribute to a child's sense of self, sexual identification, and understanding of morality. A child's

. . . .

primary experience of himself is based on his relationship with his parents. Through them, he learns who he is. He measures himself against them. Through them, he learns about similarities and differences. He learns about depending on people and about how to relate to others.

While the structure of the American family has changed radically to include millions of children growing up in single-parent families, it remains true that two loving parents provide a child with more love and affection than one. More is better. Two parents who care deeply about their child's growth and development, who are committed to their child's well-being, and who are willing to provide the emotional and financial support a child needs, give their child a distinct advantage. When parents divorce, it is important for both parents to remain actively involved in their child's life. No one is as important to a child as his two parents.

Let's say that you believe that it's important for your child to have a strong relationship with his or her other parent. If you're confused about what amount of time spent with a parent constitutes a strong relationship, you're not alone; there are no definitive answers.

In this and the following chapter, I will discuss the research and general thinking on how joint custody affects children, but first, a disclaimer about research. Whatever research is conducted on joint custody, there is always someone who will say that the research is not scientific enough, that there wasn't a control group, that the population studied was too small, that the methodology was poor, or that the population represented only middle-class people. Some reason is usually found to discredit the research. I tell you this to warn you that even with research as evidence to support your position, someone will tell you that the research was faulty. In the end, you will have to make a personal decision about whether joint custody is in your children's best interests by observing your children and by examining your own motivation and reactions.

· · · · · · · · ·

Stability

Children need stability. Joint-custody children will not find stability in the form of one house, one bed, one toothbrush, and so on. Instead, they will have to incorporate two homes, two beds, and two toothbrushes into their lives. Their sense of stability will have to come in the form of two parents who provide love and nurturing, constancy, and permanence in two separate homes, much as they did in one home before the divorce.

A child's life will be disrupted by the divorce. Since divorce is not a process geared to meet the needs of children, parents must do whatever they can to let children know that they are loved, that they will be taken care of, that there will be predictability in their lives, and that the stable force will be two loving parents.

School-age children can adapt to a variety of schedules. These children do well when their parents cooperate with each other, when they are not burdened by taking care of their parents, and when their contact with both parents is frequent and predictable.

The Preschool Child
(from birth to age four)

Young children can be very literal-minded. If you are there, you exist; if you go away, you don't exist (or you've disappeared, never to return). To feel safe, very young children need to be given a sense of trust and security in their world. They are fragile and need to feel a sense of stability, particularly in regard to who will be taking care of them. The preschool child who goes back and forth between two homes constantly fears being abandoned.

Joint custody with a preschool child requires an extraordinary amount of coordination between parents. "Every little detail—lost toys, missed naps, doctors' appointments, and so on—must be shared regularly and openly if joint custody is going to work," says Wallerstein. The timing of decisions about weaning, toilet training, entry into day care, nursery school, and other major events in the child's life must be discussed regularly by parents, suggest Rosemary McKinnon and Judith S. Wallerstein. Older children may be more flexible about bedtimes and rules that differ in each home, but a young child requires as many of the same routines as possible to have two stable environments.

Perhaps you remember a favorite object that you refused to let go of as a young child. An old blanket or teddy bear has comforted many young children. Before they are able to recall their parent in their own minds, children transfer their emotional attachment from a parent to an inanimate object, a so-called transitional object. If your preschool child has such a favorite object, allow it to go back and forth with the child between homes, to help allay your child's anxiety. Also, if you and your ex-spouse can agree on this, ask your ex-spouse to place a picture of you in your child's room in his other home. This will remind him that you are still in his life and that he will see you again in a few days.

Two separate residences mean two sets of toys, clothes, playmates —two different physical *and* psychological environments. For a young child, toys are more than playthings. They serve in fantasy play, help work out aggression, and provide security and comfort. When a young child leaves a toy at one house and finds he is missing it at the other house, it can be a major source of upset. Where toys are kept and how a child feels about them should be considered carefully.

My daughter, Deirdre, received a doll house for Chanukah from her grandmother. We asked her where she was going to keep it, at my apartment or at her father's house. She said she'd keep it at her grandmother's, because she didn't have as much to play with there. But I sensed that something was not right—that she couldn't figure out who would be offended by whatever she might decide. If she decided on my place, maybe her daddy would be hurt; or if she said his place, maybe I'd be upset. In the end, she decided to bring it to my apartment, and that was fine with her dad, too. [Cora]

. . . .

Young children need to feel secure in their relationships with their parents. They need their parents to be available to them as much as possible so that they can experience their parents' love. Preschool children living in joint-custody arrangements shouldn't spend long periods of time away from either parent. Although transition times may be difficult, the schedule I would recommend for a four-year-old would include short periods of stay with each parent, no more than two nights and three days. An alternate plan would be based on one primary home with large amounts of time spent with the other parent during the day.

"Young children pose particular problems because they need stability, continuity, and protection, because they're unable to verbalize their own needs and wishes in ways that many parents can comprehend, and because their care requires frequent communication and accord between the parents," advise McKinnon and Wallerstein. Young children often have a difficult time with joint custody because too many demands are placed on them. "Some children seem overwhelmed by the combination of changeover days, school demands, new adults brought home by parents, and many different caretaking arrangements—all in addition to the normal developmental demands of early childhood," say Wallerstein and Blakeslee in *Second Chances*.

Joint custody presents parents of young children with complex issues to manage, specifically combining the developmental needs of the child with a myriad of logistical problems. Are you up to the task? More importantly, is your child? Think about it.

The School-age Child (ages five through 12)

Gradually, school-age children take on more of the world. They learn to read, write, and master other activities. They meet classmates and their families, teachers, scout leaders, piano teachers, and sports coaches. They enjoy social events. They are able to take increasing responsibility for themselves and their lives. While a preschooler has little concept of time, a nine-year-

old can more easily master a complicated schedule of rotating
houses. For many school-age children in joint-custody
arrangements, it is a point of pride to manage themselves
and their schedules.

*Of course I know what my schedule is," says nine-year-old Greg.
"I have to know. I have to figure out what things I'll need for the
next few nights if it's a day I go to my other house. Besides, it's
fun for me to plan all that stuff.* [Greg, age 9]

Unfortunately, not all nine-year-olds can manage this well.
Some school-age children find it extremely difficult to remember
where they sleep on any given night. They never quite master the
schedule. While some children seem content just knowing who
will pick them up after school, others remain confused about their
arrangements and feel anxious about their schedules long after the
initial separation. A child's temperament has a lot to do with how
well he will adjust to joint custody.

"Children who are relatively calm and easygoing from birth
are more likely to adapt well to joint-custody arrangements," say
Wallerstein and Blakeslee. "Children who are cranky and irritable
from the start and who have trouble mastering simple routines
seem to have more trouble with joint custody, as they do with
other changes."

Some joint-custody families don't adhere to a rigid schedule.
They work it out in a more flexible manner, almost from week to
week or day by day, depending on the needs of the parents.
However, this could be tantamount to disaster for some children.
Some wouldn't be able to handle the uncertainty of not knowing
where they were going to sleep that night. Some children who
have adjusted to their routines resist changes.

*The children were eight and 11 when we separated. Our first
schedule was that they would spend one week with me and then
one week with their father. We were not rigid about sticking to that*

schedule, and both kids told us that it was especially hard when we changed things around. Then they both requested that they spend longer periods of time at each house, so that now they spend two weeks with me and two weeks with their father. It sounds easy now, but the process was a very hard one for all of us. [Lois]

Adolescents (ages 13 through 18)

Adolescence is a tumultuous time, when teenagers experience tremendous shifts in their identity, combined with many changes in their hormonal system. At times they have a tremendous desire to grow beyond the structure of the family, while at other times they have an intense desire to remain close, and so cling to the family unit. However, the central focus of their lives is not to spend time with their parents. Far from it. They want to be with their friends, and they want their friends to know where to find them.

Lauren, a teenager who has lived in a joint-custody family for many years, says that although her schedule never changed during all that time, her friends never knew where she was:

It was so foreign to them that I had two homes. I would have given a lot just to be able to say, "Here's my phone number." Not, "Here's my two phone numbers." People always looked at me like I was strange.

Adolescents crave normalcy. They want to be like everybody else—that is, like their friends. Living in two homes sets them apart. They get tired of explaining their unusual living arrangement and resent their different lifestyle. I have known many teenagers who, after living in two homes for many years, refuse to continue that arrangement. They want one home, one bed, one toothbrush, and most importantly, one phone. Life is difficult enough for them; two homes makes it that much more complicated.

. . . .

Loyalty is a major source of conflict for all children of divorce. Some teenagers who live in two homes are referred to as hyperloyal. In their desire not to offend either parent, they keep track of the extra hours they spend with one parent and make sure they even the score.

"It is more the norm to see a teenager gravitate toward living in one home on a permanent basis," says Marla Beth Isaacs, Ph.D., co-author of *The Difficult Divorce*. "If they continue living in two homes, they most likely are sacrificing themselves so as not to hurt their parents." Most teenagers want to spend as little time with their parents as possible, so to divide that small amount of time in two, to accommodate two parents living in two separate homes, may be a burden to a teenager.

Individual differences among children and their unique reactions to situations should be the guide used to determine the best custody arrangement for them. Some children are ambivalent about where they want to live. They may change their minds with some regularity, depending on whether they have had a fight with one parent, whether they are jealous of a parent's new spouse, or whether they are just tired of moving back and forth. This makes it difficult to know what is best for them.

Chelsea, a 15-year-old who has been living in two homes since she was five, has never complained about her situation. In fact, she thinks she is lucky:

Since both my parents remarried, I have four parents who love me. At my dad's house, my parents leave for work early, so I'm more independent and have to fend for myself. I get myself up in the morning, my stepbrothers and I make breakfast and lock up before we leave for school. At my mom's, my breakfast is waiting for me. Both are kind of nice.

Chelsea's adjustment to joint custody has been a smooth one. Her parents, the Gordons, have worked hard to cooperate on matters affecting their children, have not asked them to make

. . . .

difficult choices about where they wanted to live, and have established a well-ordered routine.

Learning to Live with Differences

Divorced parents spend a lot of time arguing about how the other parent parents. Joint-custody parents are even more susceptible to this debate. One parent enforces a 9 p.m. bedtime, but the other lets the child watch the 11 p.m. news. One parent insists that homework get done before any television-watching; the other (usually the same one who allows the child to watch the late news) doesn't have any rules about when homework gets done. Reviewing spelling words while watching television seems just fine. Or, since Mom is a better speller anyway, the child is encouraged to wait until he gets back to Mom's house to do his spelling homework.

Learning to live with differences is an issue for all children. Children living in intact families are very aware of their parents' differing views on child raising, since these differences cause arguments in two-parent homes as well. Children will use these differences as ammunition in the conflict between parents. ("But Mommy said I can stay up late tonight." "But Daddy said I can get a new toy tomorrow.") In two-parent homes, however, parents are more likely to join forces and settle these differences between the two of them.

When parents separate, their differences seem more pronounced. Some children learn very quickly how they should behave when they are with one parent or the other. Some rules apply in Mother's house but not in Father's. When a boy is with his father, he understands that he can behave in ways which might be unacceptable to his mother. As the differences become more obvious, some children can more easily accept the fact that in two homes there may be two sets of rules.

Is this good for a child? Not necessarily. Some children do not adjust easily to these differences. Ideally, it would be less confusing for the same set of rules to apply in two homes. No matter where the child sleeps, one bedtime is better than two, especially for a child who is very young or who seems easily confused or anxious.

Very few parents will always agree on how to deal with their children under all sets of circumstances. The more agreement about discipline and the more consistency in the routine, the better. Robert E. Adler, Ph.D., author of *Sharing the Children*, says, "...I constantly remind parents that most children can tolerate differences between their homes much more readily than hostilities between their parents."

Elaine Radiss, M.S.S., a family therapist and educator in child development, believes that the child's ability to adjust to different sets of rules comes down to "the ability of parents to keep the well-being of their child as primary at all times." Parents need to say to their children: "I know this is difficult for you. We have different rules and we agree to disagree." This helps to prevent the child from playing one parent off against the other. The acknowledgment needs to be made with the child that this is a crazy system, "but as your parents we will try not to make it any crazier for you." Of course, the better the relationship between the ex-spouses, the easier this will be to accomplish.

Kathy, age 13, says that she knows her parents do things differently:

I just take what my father has to say, and take what my mom has to say too. I know what's good and what's not, so I just take what they both have to say and I figure things out for myself.

All children sometimes work at playing one parent off against the other. Children in joint-custody families have extra ammunition: saying they want to live permanently with the other parent. Once, when my son was angry at me, he announced that he wanted to live with his father full time. I surprised myself by being fairly calm; I did not panic, noted his comment, and let the moment pass. When Sandra's daughter, Nicole, threatened her by saying she wanted to live with her Dad, Sandra's reply was, "That's a possibility." In the meantime, they had an issue to settle.

When Josh was upset with his father or me, he would want to telephone the other parent, ostensibly to complain about the bad treatment he was receiving. While neither of us appreciated the fact that Josh was trying to threaten one of us or manipulate us, as parents we had faith that we would not undermine one another. We both knew how to be open with Josh, and how to listen to him, yet we did not support his complaints about the other parent.

Parents often report confusion about whether to allow their child to escape from the argument of the moment by calling the other parent for support. While you don't want to deny access to the other parent, you can feel that the rug has been pulled out from under you when a child disappears in the midst of a disagreement to call his other parent for comfort.

In the middle of a fight with his dad, Owen often called his mother to hear her calm voice. "I know it's not right to wimp out on my dad," said Owen, "but I just need to get away from him sometimes, and the phone and a talk with my mom is the only place I can go to feel safe." Owen's mother tried to remain levelheaded and not immediately side with her son against his father. She listened to Owen and then encouraged him to go back to his dad to finish the argument. "We usually work it out," said Owen. "My dad hates it when I do that, but then, I hate it that my parents don't live in the same house." Actually, Owen's mother did what she would do if they were living in the same house—facilitating a good relationship with his dad.

Other parents allow and encourage an escape from one house to the other when times are especially rough. "I feel particularly bad when I hear my daughter is arguing with her stepmother," says one mother who shares custody with her ex-husband. "I don't mind that she calls me and wants to come over. I'm glad I'm available to her. Her life is hard enough—I couldn't possibly tell her to stick it out over there."

The result may even be harder for this daughter. While her relationship with her stepmother may be difficult, running away does not solve the problem. Everyone needs a breather from time to time, but although this mother may take some satisfaction in knowing that her daughter is in conflict with her stepmother, she needs to encourage her daughter to handle the situation more directly. If her daughter cannot do this, it would be more productive for the mother to talk to her ex-husband and his wife about the problems they are having, to see if anything can be done to resolve them.

Parents also wonder if they should call their children when they're at the other parent's house. Some children feel intruded upon and have an easier time if they are distinctly separated from one parent for a period of time. How will you feel if your ex-spouse or his new lover answers the phone? Consider telling your children you will call them at a prearranged time, or mention that they can call you.

In the beginning of our separation, I rarely called during the entire two weeks the kids were at their father's. I think now I stayed away too much. My ex-husband, on the other hand, used to call the kids every day when they were at my place, and I had to ask him to cut down on that. My daughter requested this too. She doesn't want me to call her when she's at her father's. She wants to be totally with the parent she's with for those two weeks. My son does call me occasionally, just to chat. [Lois]

Ask your children if they want you to call them when they're at their other house. Tell them how you feel about it. "How does it feel when I call you over at Dad's?" "Would you prefer I just waited to talk to you until you get back to my house?" "I miss you when I don't talk to you for a while and I imagine you feel the same way." Use every opportunity to let your children know that you realize this is hard for them, that you want to know how they feel, and that you want to do everything you can to help things go smoothly. Then be prepared to listen to their response without reacting defensively.

Transition Times

One of the greatest challenges for all joint-custody families is how to handle transition time—the time when children move from one house to the other. Transition times are difficult for all children who spend time with one parent and then another. Mothers in traditional sole-custody situations often report that their children are very difficult to live with after they return from a weekend or a day with Daddy. It takes a while to readjust to routine. Similarly, co-parents report difficulties at the time of switching from one house to another.

Early in our separation, Josh would come to my house on Sunday mornings after he had been with Jeff for three and a half days, and he usually needed some period of adjustment with me: he was not happy, he needed instant and constant attention from me, and he was generally very difficult to be with. He would calm down after a few hours, but transition times were always tense for Josh and me until the two of us eased into being with each other again. Such was not the case when Josh went to Jeff's house on Thursday afternoons. He seemed to ease into being at Jeff's house more readily, probably because he was already in the middle of a regular pattern, coming from a school afternoon and heading toward a school night before waking up the next morning to catch the bus. There was some external structure to the time when he shifted from my home to Jeff's, but very little structure when he came to my house on Sunday morning.

It took quite a while before the transition to my house became easier. We later changed our schedule so that transition times were always done through school days. The external structure helped allay everyone's anxiety about leaving one home and going to another.

Why is the transition so hard? Children often display unusual behavior. Ordinarily agreeable children become irascible, whiny, clingy, and very demanding. What are they trying to tell us? That this situation is very demanding for them. The constant separations and reunions with their parents place tremendous stress on them. They're saying that it's not a normal way to live. They are having difficulty integrating different parts of themselves, new lifestyles, expectations, and the new demands that are placed upon them.

Each transition time reminds everyone of the initial separation. Memories and old feelings resurface. Thirteen-year-old Stephanie has been going back and forth between two homes for eight years now. "Just remembering those early years brings back a lot of pain," she says. "I hate thinking about it."

Many children do become accustomed to their routines in two houses, and transition times are part of that routine. Stephanie used to strongly object when her parents would talk in front of her about how the last few days went. She didn't want to see them together because it reminded her of when they used to all live under one roof. When she was brought to Mom's house, she wanted Dad to leave right away. Her parents didn't realize this until about a year after they separated; Stephanie was young and couldn't express her needs clearly. These parents also had their own needs to be together, if only for half an hour or so. They began to talk on the phone the night before the transition day. Stephanie then had the full attention of the parent she had not seen for several days, and her unhappy behavior at transition time lessened considerably.

When Rosie's children returned to her home, she was so eager to be with them that she probably overwhelmed them with attention and questions and excitement. "They acted like I was this monster who wanted to eat them up," says Rosie. "They seemed scared of me." Rosie has learned that her children like to go up to their room and be by themselves for a while. After they've settled in and they're ready to be with her, they come downstairs. "I had to learn to go with their rhythms—not mine."

. . . .

It didn't take Monica long to realize that her daughter, Dana, became very clingy the night before a transition day. "She'd drive me crazy," says Monica. "I started to get very mad at her until I realized that she was just having a hard time letting go of me." It was hard on Monica, too. She didn't like the idea of letting her little girl go. Instead of resisting Dana's difficult behavior, Monica began to allow extra time at bedtime for talking, hugs, special music, and stories. "We made it a time we both looked forward to, and it stopped being such a heavy thing for both of us."

Children often feel that they lead two distinct lives, and the symbol of this division is the time they move from one house to the other. No wonder it's difficult! The continual adjustments that children and their parents are forced to make because of living in two homes need to be considered with sensitivity and careful planning. It takes time. Some children adjust to their routine within six months or a year. Others are not comfortable with moving back and forth for years. Still others never become accustomed to the endless moves. In the poignant words of one ten-year-old boy, "I went from having one home to two homes, but it feels like I have no home."

A fact of joint custody is that children have two distinct residences. A child in this situation needs to deal with what it means to have two homes. It is probably different from the way most of his friends live. All children whose parents are living apart need to respond to their friends' questions about the absent parent. One child I know never told his friends at his dad's house that he had a mom—he kept her existence to himself. Children have to tell their friends where to call them on what days, and they have to explain why they get on the school bus at a different stop on Friday mornings.

I overheard a conversation my son had with a friend who wanted to know where Jeff was and why he wasn't living with us any more. Josh answered that his parents weren't happy living together, that Jeff lived nearby, and then said, "I'm tired of this discussion—let's play."

"It's hard for me to explain to my friends," says 11-year-old Sean:

I tell them that my mother and father live in different houses and that I go to their house every half a week. And they say, "Oh yeah?" Most of the people that I'm telling, their parents live together. So it's hard to explain, 'cause they're not used to it. To me, though, it's not joint custody or anything like that. It's just a family.

Reunions

Most children of divorce wish their parents would get back together again. No matter how unhappy their parents' marriage was, no matter how much fighting there was, children do not like the fact that their parents have divorced. Six-year-old Kim says, "When my daddy comes to my mommy's house to pick us up, I hope he'll just stay and we never have to leave each other again." There is always the potential for a reuniting of the family. The reality of the separation and the loss is so painful that for years to come, children may construct fantasies of a happy family life. Ask your children if they ever think of you and their other parent getting back together again. Their answers will be revealing.

What about joint-custody children? Many of their parents talk to each other frequently and may even celebrate holidays and special events together. Doesn't this increase the potential for fantasies of reuniting as a family? Yes, it might. You still might decide to spend time together as a family. If you make your intentions clear to your children, you might help them see a family outing for what it is—a chance for all of you to be together and enjoy each other's company, not a prelude to marital reconciliation.

Ask your children how they feel about the family being together for special occasions. Some children do react negatively when their parents spend short periods of time together during transitions. During those times, your child doesn't get your undivided attention. Also, what if your child thinks you're making plans to get back together again? Shouldn't that be avoided at all costs?

Some people say that children should get used to the fact that their parents are no longer married and that when parents spend time together they are feeding a child's fantasies of reconciliation. This seems like a rather rigid approach to me. Both parents and children can enjoy some times together without harming the children. Some children look forward to these times and years later remember them with great fondness as times when their parents, despite their personal difficulties, were able to come together to be parents to their child. I'm sure you've felt that no one cares as much about your child as you and his other parent does. Your child feels this too.

In the years following our separation, Josh and Jeff and I have spent some very pleasant times together. Not at my house, which reminded Josh of the years when we all lived there together, but in some neutral territory which Josh helped choose, such as a restaurant or school function. We always celebrated Josh's birthday together and have come together for major events in his life such as his bar mitzvah and high-school graduation, with much pride in our son and in our ability to cooperate fully as parents to him.

The three of us did go out to dinner once, and Julie loved it. And it was a chance for Jim and me to get caught up on stuff. And in fact we were talking about adult stuff, not Julie-related stuff. And she said, "Listen, you people are here to take me out to dinner, so you talk to me!" But when I pushed for us to do that again, and it was easy for us all to have lunch together at her day-care center, Jim said no. And the reason that he gave was that he thought that would get Julie's expectations up about us getting back together again. I don't think that was the real reason. I think that it was still hard for him to be with me and maybe it was painful in the sense of reminding him too much of the family that we had.

. . . .

For Julie's birthday the next year Jim came to my house and my parents and sisters were there. Julie loved it. She felt that her people had come together for her and she was really clear that at the end of the day Jim was going to go home to his house. I think when she said, "I'd like you to get back together," she knew that was not going to happen, she was just expressing that feeling. [Charlotte]

Sometimes children specifically request their parents not to attend the same function together. Although there is only one official visiting day at camp, Chelsea asked her parents, who had both remarried, not to come together. It was just too much for her to manage. Her parents granted her request, and her father made arrangements with the camp to see Chelsea the following weekend.

My son asked Jeff and me not to show up with our new spouses for parents' weekend at his college. Four parents and a new baby half sister was just too much for him to cope with. I also wonder if he wasn't embarrassed by the idea of this unusual show of family (albeit divorced family) togetherness. My husband and I stayed home that weekend and visited him another time.

Josh's elementary school sponsored an annual Spring Thing, which we all attended together for several years. Since this is a time when families are together, it seemed reasonable for Josh to want both his parents with him, and Jeff and I wanted to be part of that experience. Any discomfort that Josh previously had with the three of us being together didn't occur any more. When it was time for us to leave the event, he would go off with the parent he came with, did not ask for the time to be extended, and he behaved in an entirely appropriate way throughout our time together. It was good for Jeff, Josh, and me to spend some informal times together. We never pretended that we were like any other family at a family outing. But in a way, I guess we were. We were two parents who loved their child very much and a child who loved being with his parents—in the same place, at the same time.

· · · · · · · · · ·

Aches and Pains

I have a headache and a tummyache a lot of the time. My teacher says it's because I'm hurting inside. [Kevin, age seven]

Many children whose parents separate often complain of aches and pains.

Soon after Jeff and I separated, Josh began to tell me that his brain hurt, or that he felt weak. After a while this pattern subsided, and another kind of behavior developed. It seemed that whenever Jeff would go away on a trip and our schedule changed somewhat, Josh would get sick—not just a cold, but a high fever of 104 or 105 degrees, and occasionally a case of strep throat. It took time for me to make the connection between Jeff's absence and Josh's illnesses.

I began to talk to Josh about what I thought was happening, saying that I noticed that he got sick whenever Dad went away. He agreed that he did. I didn't interpret why this was so. I did notice, though, that Josh's illnesses decreased considerably as he became more comfortable with and secure in our living situation. When he had enough experience to see that Jeff always came back, he stopped getting sick when Jeff went away. Like many children adjusting to a new, complicated lifestyle, in time Josh became more flexible about schedules, vacations, and an individual parent's temporary absence.

How do most children who live in joint-custody arrangements behave? Many divorced parents with traditional custody arrangements say that their children show a greater sense of independence. Single parents need help from their children in order to accomplish the daily tasks of living, so they encourage their children to be self-reliant. Joint-custody parents report the same kind of behavior in their children.

Years ago, I talked with a close friend who spoke about some characteristics of Josh's that she thought were unusual. "He's much more worldly-wise than most kids his age. He can negotiate his way in strange places, handle money well, and talks to adults in a mature way." Were these characteristics a result of joint custody or of who Josh was and would be no matter what his lifestyle? It was hard to know. She described Josh as much more mature and independent than most children his age, and worried that he had grown up too fast. "Where's his childhood?" she wondered.

This is a concern for many joint-custody parents. Their children are given responsibilities seemingly well beyond their years, and for the most part, they manage well. Parents are grateful when their children master their schedules, pack up their belongings to get ready for transition time, deliver important messages to the other parent, and, for the most part, don't complain about their complex living arrangements.

As children move through stages of development, old feelings of uncertainty about their lives may return. This is a natural part of accepting and adjusting to their way of life. Children can get angry with you all over again for having separated. They may become as depressed and withdrawn as when you first separated. Adolescents may ask questions about your divorce, whether one of you had an affair, or why your divorce was necessary. They will have their own opinions about how you've lived your life, and can make discussions about family relationships quite unpleasant. Children need time to deal with all the feelings brought on by their parents' separation and divorce, as well as feelings they have about how their parents have chosen to continue parenting.

Is it asking a lot to want children to accept living in two different places? I think so. But there are benefits. Living at two residences allows a child whose parents have separated to relate to each of his parents continually and to know both of them intimately. Children with the least problems following divorce were those who had a good individual relationship with each parent after divorce, according to a research study by R.D. Hess and K.A. Camara and published in the *Journal of Social Issues*. Children living in a joint-custody situation often become extremely close to both parents. Relationships become stronger as a result of a more intimate interaction between parent and child. There is no one to interfere, and no one to take over for you in a tense situation. Parents report feeling closer to their children after their separation, since the time they spend together is more concentrated.

Parents—all separated parents—need to trust themselves, each other, and their children. You need to look at your children, to hear what they are saying, and to understand what their behavior is saying. You also need to think clearly about what behavior is age-appropriate and what might be related to a separation or divorce in the family. (For example, nightmares are common at ages four and five, and may not signal fears of abandonment because you have divorced.)

Children need the time and opportunity to express their feelings in whatever way is comfortable for them, and to accept those feelings. If you are having difficulty sorting out your own feelings and find it hard to listen to your children, a professional can help. A trained family therapist or counselor will be able to support you as you move through the difficult process of divorce.

A child's adjustment to separation and divorce in general, and to joint custody in particular, does not happen overnight. Many children, as well as adults, need years to come to terms with their new lives. However, many children are able to take control of their new way of life with greater speed and flexibility than you might imagine.

Children who can continue their relationships with both parents after divorce and children whose parents cooperate in raising them are likely to fare better. Children who can be flexible with a complex set of arrangements often learn their schedules easily, are clear about the times they go to each home, and are able to explain the way they live to their friends. While they may wish their parents would live together again, like most children whose parents have separated or divorced, they understand that this will not happen. They also understand that with joint custody, they can continue their loving relationship with both parents.

· · · · · · · · ·

As Chelsea says, "Living in joint custody means both parents love me and both want to be with me. That's why they have joint custody."

5

What Do the Professionals Say?

Is joint custody good for children? It depends. It depends on whom you ask, whose research you study, and, primarily, your own beliefs.

When I wrote the first edition of this book 12 years ago, there was little research to substantiate the beliefs of professionals in the field. Since then further research has been done, but it is controversial. Some studies have been done with a clinical population—that is, people who were receiving counseling in social-service agencies for help in adjusting to postdivorce life. Other studies were done with volunteers who were recruited through newspaper ads, friends, teachers, and clergy. For every study indicating that children are content with joint-custody arrangements, another indicates that many of them are unhappy, exhibiting behavior problems, and doing poorly in school.

In this chapter, I will present some of the professionally held opinions on and research about joint custody, but be warned: you will not find in these pages a definitive answer to the question, "Is joint custody good for children?"

One Primary Parent—Or Two?

In 1973, a book was written to help the courts develop guidelines for child placement and child custody decisions. In their book *Beyond the Best Interests of the Child*, which I'll refer to as *BBIC*, Joseph Goldstein, Anna Freud, and Albert Solnit created quite a controversy in the professional community. Their position was that when parents cannot agree on custody, the court should award custody to the child's psychological parent; that is, only one parent. The psychological parent is the primary caretaker, the person the child views as the main parent. The authors felt that if parents could not agree on custody, children should not have to deal with the ambiguities of a relationship with a noncustodial parent.

"Children have difficulty in relating positively to, profiting from, and maintaining contact with two psychological parents who are not in positive contact with each other," the authors wrote. "Loyalty conflicts are common and normal under such conditions and may have devastating consequences by destroying the child's positive relationships to both parents." Further, the authors argued that this psychological parent should be the only parent to make decisions concerning the child, including how often and even *if* the child would have contact with the noncustodial parent.

The response to *BBIC* was strong and fairly consistent. In my 1978 book, I wrote that children of divorce need to feel loved, valued, and cared for by both parents. They need to know that even if a parent moves out of the house, this does not mean that the parent is moving out of their lives. I asserted that children have a right to a relationship with both parents, and could not successfully adjust to divorce without it. That same year Mel

Roman and William Haddad, authors of *The Disposable Parent*, also criticized *BBIC*. They cited its lack of ". . .social-service data to support the proposition that a single official parent is preferable to two. . . ."

In addition, *BBIC* was strongly criticized by the Group for the Advancement of Psychiatry Committee on the Family. In its 1981 report, as quoted in Philip M. Stahl's "A Review of Joint and Shared Parenting Literature," the Committee wrote:

> The relationships with mother and father constitute an emotional universe for the child. If, in the crisis of divorce, one part of that universe is cut off, labeled as bad, and becomes unavailable, there will be adverse consequences for the child's view of himself and of the people he will relate to later in life.

Other criticisms of *BBIC* centered on the control exercised by the mother (who would most often be the psychological parent) concerning the father's visitation. If the mother was angry and wanted to keep the father away, this would damage the relationship between father and child. The question to be answered was, "If the father is not declared the psychological parent, is his relationship with his child worth protecting?"

Early studies said yes. In *Surviving the Breakup*, Wallerstein and Kelly described a five-year study of 60 families in Marin County, California. Their findings pointed to the importance of continued relationships with both parents. The sense of loss felt by divorced children was eased when fathers were more involved in their children's lives. Wallerstein and Kelly wrote, ". . .divorcing parents should be encouraged and helped to shape postdivorce arrangements which permit and foster continuity in the children's relations with both parents."

Other studies pointed to children's yearning for contact with their fathers after divorce. In her research, E. Mavis Hetherington found that postdivorce father-child relationships could not be

. . . .

predicted on the basis of the pre-divorce relationship. That is, a father who, prior to divorce, was not involved in his child's life could, in fact, become a loving, active parent after the divorce.

Family therapist Paula Rosen, Ph.D., in her unpublished doctoral dissertation, "A Study of Joint-Custody Families," found "...the continued involvement of both parents in the child's daily life was shown to reduce significantly the trauma of divorce for all family members." Other early studies by Susan Steinman and Alice Abarbanel found that joint custody reduced the emotional stress and sense of loss brought on by divorce and that children felt strongly attached to both parents.

The research further indicated that fathers were faring well in joint-custody arrangements. Harry F. Keshet and Kristine M. Rosenthal wrote in "Fathering After Marital Separation" that fathers who had joint custody had full and rich relationships with their children. In "Fathers, Children and Joint Custody," Judith Brown Greif found that fathers who were forced into a secondary parenting position see themselves less and less as parents "...and eventually act in accordance with the role that had been assigned to them: the absent parent." Fathers who had joint custody, on the other hand, were more likely to remain actively involved in all aspects of their children's lives, to the benefit of all concerned.

Joint custody appeared to be providing children with easy and continuing access to both parents. These early studies also highlighted the children's sense of well-being, their overall satisfaction with a two-household living arrangement, and the fact that they experienced the ongoing love of both parents. In several studies all the children living in joint-custody families said that if given the choice, they would choose to continue their living arrangements. They were pleased that their parents cared enough about them to agree on joint custody.

Yet there were indications that switching back and forth between two homes was too cumbersome for some children. These children were confused, anxious, and frustrated as they attempted to carry out their lives in two separate households.

Rosemary McKinnon and Judith S. Wallerstein, in "A Preventive Intervention Program for Parents and Children in Joint-Custody Arrangements," reported that younger children had an especially difficult adjustment. A significant minority of children studied experienced hyperloyalty and feelings of being overburdened. Other problems reported in the literature centered on the amount of hard work involved in managing complicated arrangements, especially just after divorce. Parents reported differing views on how much contact they wanted with the other parent, how to work out questions of conflicting lifestyles, and how to handle finances.

Even with the problems described, the idea of joint custody— both parents cooperating and remaining active as parents, the schedule working smoothly, and the child adjusting well—was seen as the best alternative. No study suggested that joint custody would eliminate children's pain and distress after divorce. But taken as a whole, the studies indicated that when joint custody was working well, it served the needs of children and their parents.

Joint Custody and Joint Decisions

Then something shifted. Because of some early studies pointing to the benefits of joint custody, especially for fathers, as well as pressure from noncustodial fathers who felt excluded from their children's lives, many states began to enact new joint-custody legislation. Writing in *Family and Conciliation Courts Review*, Sheila James Kuehl stated that fathers' rights organizations worked quickly and easily to convince male legislators and judges that without such new legislation, ". . .vindictive ex-wives could unfairly restrict their access to their children." In 1978, only 13 states had joint-custody legislation on the books. By 1989, 33 states had some type of joint-custody statute, either as an option for contested custody cases or as the preferred solution. (See Chapter 6 for more detail.)

The result was that joint custody no longer became an arrangement just for parents who agreed on it themselves. It was court-ordered in record numbers, even over the objection of individual parents, and even when parents showed animosity toward each other. How could such parents ever cooperate in raising their children? The prevailing notion was that they would just have to try. Although courts could not legislate goodwill, people thought that over time, hostilities would cease and the parents' concern for their children would serve to unite them in making arrangements in a more amicable manner. Unfortunately, in many cases it has not worked out that way.

More recent studies have looked at families in which joint custody was court-ordered. Bitterness still characterizes many of the relationships between parents, and the children are caught in their parents' wars as they go back and forth between two homes.

Most professionals are vehemently opposed to court-ordered joint custody and tell horrifying tales of families in which the joint custody solution seems like a nightmare. I worked with one family in which the father had minimal contact with his children for eight years after his divorce. Then he asked the court for joint custody, and it was awarded. The children, barely knowing of his existence, did not want to spend time with a stranger, even if he was their father. The mother, clearly the psychological parent and for the past eight years the sole emotional and financial provider for these children, was stunned by the change.

Some professionals have changed their views on joint custody. Deborah Luepnitz, Ph.D., supported joint custody in her 1982 book *Child Custody: A Study of Families After Divorce.* But now she favors the primary caretaker presumption, similar to the position taken in *BBIC.* Luepnitz is among those who have seen formerly uninvolved fathers sue their ex-wives for joint custody, seemingly just to harass them—and win. One father who abandoned his son soon after the child was born would appear sporadically to spend some time with his son. During these visits he was abusive to his wife. Then he would disappear again for long periods. When the boy was five, his father petitioned the court for visitation rights and won. The child was frightened of his father and had bad memories of his previous visits. Subsequently the father fought for joint custody and won, and the time allotments he was awarded increased with the years. The child was afraid to go to his father's house and, on several occasions, the father called the police to force his son to come along. (Ultimately a judge stopped him from doing this.) Dr. Luepnitz believes that judges reward fathers too much for showing any interest at all in their children. "The revolution should not start after divorce," Dr. Luepnitz says.

Other professionals unfavorable to court-ordered joint custody include Sam Kirschner, Ph.D., a family therapist and co-author of *Comprehensive Family Therapy.* Dr. Kirschner says that even under ideal circumstances—which he has seen in less than ten percent of divorced families—joint custody is a source of tremendous aggravation and pain. When parents are at war, he finds that joint-custody arrangements are "insane, conducted by disturbed people," and that children become emotionally and developmentally paralyzed at this traumatic time in their lives.

Richard A. Gardner, M.D., author of many books about divorce, writes in *Family Evaluation in Child-Custody Litigation* that one of the important criteria for awarding joint custody is that "the parents prove that they are able to cooperate in the joint-custodial arrangements; [they] must demonstrate the capacity to communicate well, and be willing to make the compromises necessary to insure the viability of the arrangements."

In Gardner's experience, most people battling for custody are not able to cooperate in childrearing activities even after the dispute is settled. Further, he finds that instead of a joint-custodial arrangement, these parents have a *no-custodial arrangement*:

> Neither parent has power or control, and the children find themselves in a no-man's-land, exposed to the crossfire of the parents, pulled apart like rope in a tug-of-war, and available as weapons for both sides. The likelihood of children developing psychopathology in such situations approached the 100 percent level.

· · · · · · · · ·

In an important study done at the Center for the Family in Transition in Corte Madera, California, J.R. Johnston and colleagues wrote that when parents were still disputing, even after a mediated settlement or a court order of joint custody, "...children who had more frequent access were more emotionally troubled and behaviorally disturbed." These children "...were significantly more depressed, withdrawn and uncommunicative, had more somatic symptoms and tended to be more aggressive...." Parents seemed to argue more when their children had more frequent access arrangements, "...although the intensity of their discord diminished with time." The authors strongly caution "...against encouraging or mandating joint custody or frequent access when parents are in ongoing disputes."

Wallerstein and Blakeslee agree, stating in *Second Chances* that "simple solutions do not work in complicated situations like bitterly contested divorces." They and others working in the field of divorce had hoped that involving fathers in parenting would decrease the acrimony between parents. That hasn't happened. It seems that "...a joint-custody arrangement to which both parents do not submit voluntarily may not be the answer; there is no evidence that joint custody is best for all, or even for most, families," she writes.

Most clinicians see the effects of court-ordered joint custody in their offices. Marla Isaacs, Ph.D., co-author of *The Difficult Divorce*, has found that in these situations—what she calls "bad joint custody"—the children suffer a great deal. She has told me that "Crucial decisions get put off for eight months or more because parents are unable to decide, and then a judge has to get involved." Dr. Isaacs has counseled families whose decisions about schooling were put off—and even children who needed to take medicine for an attention-deficit disorder, but who were not receiving medicine because the parents couldn't agree. "Kids don't wait just because parents do," says Dr. Isaacs.

SaraKay Cohen Smullens, a family therapist and the author of *Whoever Said Life Is Fair?*, feels strongly that joint custody is not in the best interest of very young children or teenagers, especially when parents cannot cooperate. "When long-term betrayal and helplessness to resolve differences occur, and when the negotiation between the partners doesn't begin to heal these deepest of wounds, but instead exacerbates them, emotions run the gamut between rage and hatred," Smullens writes. When a court awards joint custody, hoping that parents will rise to the occasion and communicate effectively, they rarely do. Smullens asserts that putting children in the middle of this ongoing warfare can be disastrous for the children.

The Main Concerns

Whether it is voluntary or court-ordered, joint custody has always been the object of criticism. These are the major arguments used to oppose joint custody:

- Children need one home and one primary parent.
- Children need roots. Joint custody inhibits them from developing a sense of stability.
- Joint custody is very confusing to children. They cannot cope with switching back and forth between two homes.
- Children who grow up in a joint-custody situation will have problems experiencing intimacy later in their lives.
- Joint custody is a manipulation by ex-spouses to stay in touch with each other so that they can continue a destructive relationship. Joint custody does not allow parents to really separate from each other.

I would like to address each of these objections individually.

"Children need one home."

Many mental-health professionals familiar with postdivorce family life feel strongly that children need one primary parent in one home, and that any other arrangement is destructive to a child's sense of self and emotional well-being. Many professionals contend that after separation and divorce, children need to establish continuity of relationship with one parent. This cannot happen successfully if they routinely move from one home to another and from an emotional connection with one parent to an emotional connection with the other.

The basic question is, can children have an emotional connection with a parent in one home and an emotional connection with another parent in another home? I believe they can. Undeniably, children's lives are disrupted by their parents' divorce. But I think the disruption is greater if they have to stop relating to one parent completely—usually the father. If this occurs, they are plagued with questions about the absent parent: "Where did my father go?" "Why don't I see him like I used to?" "Doesn't he love me?" "I miss my Daddy."

Joint custody can provide a structure for both parent and child to maintain a continuing relationship, perhaps one even closer than before. When joint custody works well, children do not have difficulty relating to both parents. Many children talk about how much they value their relationships with both parents and understand there is something special in those relationships. Children report seeing more of their parents, especially their fathers, than before the separation. Many find that they spend more time with their fathers than friends who live in intact families.

If parents have difficulty relating to each other, children will probably experience difficulty in relating to each parent. Children look to their parents as role models for relating to people in general. One 12-year-old girl whose divorced parents cooperate well told me, "Being with my mom half the time and my dad half the time makes me feel more grateful for them both."

In order for children to feel secure living in two homes, they need a clear sense of what is expected of them in each one. They need to be told that there may be different rules and different standards of behavior. Children usually learn quickly what is appropriate in different living environments and are usually able to adapt to that without any problem. The important thing is for parents to talk openly about these differences with their children. Problems arise when their parents are unhappy about the differences. It is their anger or their acceptance that sets the tone for how the children will adjust to differences.

"Children need roots."

Joint custody prevents children from developing a sense of stability, some say. Critics of joint custody contend that children who are constantly shifted from one home to another have no sense of belonging anywhere. They never establish roots, rarely experience security, and fail to develop trust in their environment. Children, they contend, cannot learn to be autonomous and capable unless they have a solid home base. This means one solid home, not two.

Edith Atkin and Estelle Rubin, co-authors of *Part-Time Father*, state:

> Children need a base that is home. . . . This insistence
> that the children should believe they have two homes
> only emphasizes that they live in a divided world. [The
> father's] home can be a place where they feel
> comfortable, accepted, loved—in short, where they feel
> at home. But their home is at their mother's.

Obviously, these authors are describing a situation in which the mother has custody of the children and the father has visitation rights, but they feel strongly that *any* form of shared custody is a bad idea.

Paula Rosen, Ph.D., a family therapist whose joint-custody study was mentioned earlier, asserted in a personal interview that "the key issue is not how many homes a child has, but his relationship with each parent and the parents' relationship with each other." One home or two, intact or divorced family, if the parents are struggling and angry, the child will not experience a sense of stability.

Many children establish roots very well in two homes. Before separation they had roots in their relationships with both parents. After the separation, the roots took hold firmly and flourished through the joint-custody arrangement. It is up to the parents to create stability for their children, which can be done in a variety of ways. Given a friendly or even neutral relationship between parents who can cooperate in raising the children, stability can develop for the children. It is knowledge that the parent-child relationship is secure which creates the child's sense of stability. Joint custody enhances this sense. There are no wrenchings, no major breaks in the child's emotional ties with either parent. Says Robert E. Adler, Ph.D., in *Sharing the Children*: "For children of divorce, real stability can only be guaranteed by parents who agree to and abide by a reasonable and fair parenting plan."

Continuity is enhanced when divorced parents live near each other, so their children can go to school from either home and can easily maintain their social life from both homes. For children between the ages of seven and 12, maintaining peer relationships is especially important.

Parents can provide continuity for younger children by helping them master their schedules, as well as by being available and predictable. It is interesting to note, however, that while some children will say they have two homes so as not to upset either parent, they actually feel that they have one primary home and a second home where they feel comfortable. This is especially true of children who still live in the original family home and whose parents live near each other. Often I've seen joint-custody children who leave most of their clothes and belongings at one home, which they use as a base of operations. This just seems simpler to them.

In my experience, when joint-custody arrangements are compatible with all family members, many children have found stability in these arrangements. They know their schedules precisely, are in strong command of their living situations, and, most important, know they can count on their parents. Other children never seem to feel secure in a second home. They may feel awkward in being with one parent's new spouse or with stepsiblings, or they may not have good friends in their new neighborhood. Living in two homes does not work for everyone. Each child is unique, and the same solution will not work for all of them.

"Joint custody is confusing to children."

Critics of joint custody believe that children cannot cope with switching back and forth between two homes. They believe that a child should be able to say, "This is my bedroom. These are my books. When I do my homework tonight, this is where I'll sit." The bedroom must be the same bedroom every night, and the books must be in the same place every night; any other arrangement increases the trauma of divorce for children, critics claim. They contend that uniformity eases the pain of separation and divorce, and children who grow up in two homes experience a great deal of confusion which then leads to emotional disturbance.

Some parents I have spoken with say that their children were somewhat confused in the first few months of establishing the joint-custody arrangement, but that this confusion lessened fairly quickly. Some studies report that 25 to 30 percent of children in joint custody experienced confusion about their living arrangements. Other parents report that their children have never seemed confused by their living arrangements. If confusion does exist, it can often be minimized by a regular schedule. Many children quickly learn their schedules and impress their parents and others around them with their ability to know just where they belong on what days. Other children, however, never quite master their routine.

It has always amazed me that my daughter, since the age of four when we separated, has always known what her schedule is.

Sure we told her, and it's never basically changed, but she's nine now and she's never had to ask me, 'What day is today? Where am I going tonight?' She's been in control of that from day one. [Marylou]

I have known many children who live in two homes and are not confused. Certainly they forget things, as all children do, but they are not, by nature, confused children. These children say to themselves, in one way or another and with the help of their parents, "I am still me. These are still my parents. I have a desk and a bed and books in two homes." The clearer the parents are about the living arrangements, and the more certainty they have about the workability of the joint-custody system, the less confusion the child will experience.

I do not mean to minimize concerns about the need for stability in children's lives. Separation and divorce are confusing for everyone and represent a time filled with instability and uncertainty. The key question is what will best help children adjust to this new family life. Will your children's needs be best served by staying in one home or moving back and forth between two homes? It is not always easy to know. What the professionals do know is that life is much easier for children after a divorce when their parents do not battle one another and trap their children in the middle.

"Children who grow up in joint custody will have problems experiencing intimacy later in their lives."

The potential problem relates not just to a joint-custody situation, but to all situations in which parents have formed new relationships.

Suppose A and B have a child and then divorce; A and C marry; B and D marry. How many adults does the child now relate to as parent figures? What if A and C, or B and D, later divorce? How many sets of grandparents will the child have? What impact will these changes have on the child's ability to form intimate relationships? With so many adults in his life, does a child relate to them less closely than if he had only two parents?

There is no question that the more adults there are in a child's life, the greater the potential for complications, difficulties, and loyalty conflicts. It would be most unusual for a child never to experience a conflict with his parent's new mate. All these relationships can be terribly upsetting for children, and stepfamily relationships are especially fraught with difficulty. The question is how these conflicts and these relationships are managed—not necessarily how many people there are in a child's life.

I believe that the number of people in a child's life should not be equated with his capacity for intimacy. Being close to more people does not diminish a child's capacity for intimacy. What does diminish a child's capacity for intimacy is not having intimate relationships early in life with the primary caretakers. Even if a child relates to only two parents, he will not necessarily be free of problems with intimacy. Most people have trouble with intimacy at some time. If A and B, A and C, and B and D all relate to a child with warmth and love—while A and B continue to provide the primary parenting—I think that child will have a rich life and positive outlook. She will learn that she can be close to several adults and find her needs met, not just by her parents, but by others as well.

"Joint custody is a manipulation that does not allow parents to really separate from each other."

According to this objection, joint custody represents an inability of parents to let go, which prevents them from establishing individual lives for themselves. Critics argue that joint custody perpetuates a destructive relationship between ex-spouses and provides the two adults with a structure for continuing their battles.

In *Part-Time Father*, Atkin and Rubin maintain that what they call divided custody "clearly. . .has more to do with the parents' need to keep their own fighting relationship going than with the child's best interests."

The most unhappy children I have seen in my office have been those whose parents have never stopped arguing. This is true whether they live in one home or two. If parents are fighting, they can fight in a sole- or joint-custody arrangement, and in either case the children are well aware of the conflict. As a result, they have no peace or sense of stability, and they cannot look forward to a future when relations will ease. They are constantly being asked, in one way or another, to choose sides. Years go by and still there is no letup. In joint-custody families, frequent contact exacerbates bitter relations.

I have worked with members of families in court-ordered joint-custody arrangements who are as angry at each other today as they were when they divorced years ago. In these situations I sometimes suggest that the parents stop trying to make arrangements with each other at all and let the adolescent children do their own negotiating. This is not a happy solution, but it does eliminate some tension between parents. Is it fair to the children? No. But likewise it is unfair for them to have parents who have not learned to put aside their bitterness as a courtesy to their children.

Constance R. Ahrons, Ph.D., the Associate Director of the Marriage and Family Program at the University of Southern California and co-author with Roy H. Rogers of *Divorced Families*, points out: "Divorce doesn't end family relationships, it redefines them." Many parents with joint custody choose to redefine their relationship as that of two parents who continue to love and care for their children. They may dislike each other, and they may even have fantasies of harming one another, but they do not intend to harm their children, and they behave accordingly.

Is there such a thing as a healthy divorce, and if so, what is it like? The healthy resolution of a relationship which has ended in divorce consists of being able to say that the marital union is over and maintaining some of the good parts to the relationship. Some who choose shared parenting might stay close to each other in a way that does not produce growth and change for both of them. But this need not be the case. People *can* learn to live with their ambivalent feelings in a relationship, and they can use those feelings to learn about themselves and their behavior.

For those couples who do not have children, totally severing the relationship can be relatively easy. It may not be so easy if children are involved, but certainly it would be easier if joint custody were not the chosen option. In any case, parents must learn to tolerate ambivalence and conflicting feelings. Cutting oneself off from an ex-spouse might mean not being able to tolerate those parts of oneself seen in the other. It also means not being able to continue experiencing what was good in the relationship, such as a shared appreciation of and interest in your children. Why should that come to an end, now that the parents are living apart? There is no reason that it should. The decision to have joint custody should be determined first on the basis of the children's needs. An added benefit can be parents maintaining a sense of connectedness and family, in a constructive, healthy way.

Our society has a lot of structure and rules: either two people are in a marriage or they are not; a child has a home or does not; a person has a family or does not. Humans need rules, but I believe the need for rules are sometimes understood in a limited way. It would be helpful to establish broader views of what constitutes a family. Before I remarried, my son and I were a family. Our family also included my parents, my brother and his family, aunts, uncles and cousins, and our many friends. They all provided us with nurturing and a feeling that we belonged together. A joint-custodial relationship allows ex-spouses to maintain the parent system that was part of their marriage in whatever way feels comfortable to them.

While many parents who have joint custody have some difficulties in getting along, they generally respect and appreciate the other parent. They feel glad, for the most part, that they are not parenting alone. Many parents with whom I have spoken feel grateful for the help and support of their ex-mate. These parents have been able to work out their differences well enough to share parenting of their children.

In our early years of joint custody, I do remember times when Jeff and I had trouble getting through our business because each of us seemed to have hidden agendas. Mine was making Jeff feel guilty, and his was reacting to my guilt-inducing behavior and fighting to maintain his parental equality. We definitely had our struggles. As the years went by, however, we learned to watch for potential trouble spots and to conduct our negotiations in a spirit of cooperation and goodwill.

It has meant a lot to me to be able to show my son that his father and I are committed to his well-being. We talked about his needs, negotiated with fairness and flexibility, and provided him with a sense of family. I like to believe that our postdivorce family life has enhanced Josh's definition of love.

The Opportunities

More than any other custody arrangement, joint custody gives individuals an opportunity to be independent adults. Although it is sometimes the case, it is a basic misunderstanding to think that joint custody forces people to stay locked into a childish relationship with each other, or that it prevents people from being able to make independent life choices.

Joint custody is sometimes criticized because it restricts people's freedom to move, either because of remarriage or job opportunities. I have always chosen where I wanted to live, and I chose to live close to Jeff so that Josh could have a primary relationship with both of us. I did not choose to be apart from Josh, and I did not choose for Josh to be apart from his father. That decision was made out of strength, not weakness.

Joint custody and the child-free time I did have allowed me to make more of a life for myself than any other custodial arrangement would have (unless Jeff had had sole custody, which would have denied me the role of an active, involved parent).

In her article "The Best of Both Parents," Charlotte Baum, co-parent of three children, responded to the view of dependency between ex-spouses in a joint-custody situation:

> Some psychologists cautioned us that the frequent contact our situation demands would be a way for us to avoid making a complete break and to continue a husband-wife dependence that in their eyes was illegitimate. The argument still puzzles me because I wonder how we could sever our ties with each other when we have children in common who will remain a constant in our lives. Our dependency on each other, if that is the proper term, is centered on the children. We do not turn to each other for comfort when we have personal problems. We do rely upon each other to take over in some situations, to help out when the children are involved. . .Joint custody doesn't create an artificial bond; children link you forever.

Is there such a thing as a friendly or cooperative divorce, in the true sense of the term, in which each parent truly has an equal voice in raising the children? In some instances, yes. It is not a concept that can be forced, however. In the years following a separation, most parents feel angry, hurt, bitter, betrayed, and terribly disappointed. Friendliness is not foremost in their hearts. In time, however, many couples can learn to be civil with each other so that their children are cared for by the two people who love them the most.

Is joint custody the best solution for your child? There is no clear-cut formula which would determine the answer to this question, given each unique situation and each unique child. What is known, as Wallerstein pointed out in her keynote address to the 1988 Spring Conference of The Association of Family and Conciliation Courts, is this: ". . .joint physical custody requires

· · · · · · · · · ·

parental commitment to the plan, a capacity to live with difference and ambiguity, and flexibility and cooperation on the part of the child." Does this sound like your family? If so, then you might be able to make joint custody work—but be prepared for the fact that it *will* take a great deal of work.

6

The Law

*Joint custody is not even heavily debated in family law.
The general feeling is that it's better to have one
custodial parent and good visitation for the other
parent.* —Gary Skoloff, chairman,
Family Law Section of the
American Bar Association

Joint custody has always been heavily debated among
practitioners and observers of family law. Not long ago, only a few
states had joint-custody statutes. Now states have statutes that
recognize the arrangement, and the vast majority of these states
allow joint custody to be ordered over the objections of one
parent. Sixteen states prefer some form of joint custody to all other
custody arrangements.

The debate, far from receding, seems to be getting more heated, with the result that states have amended their joint-custody legislation. Fathers'-rights organizations, which were in the forefront of lobbying for joint-custody legislation, now find themselves opposing advocates for women who believe that joint-custody laws are eroding their influence as parents. Most lawyers and judges seem to agree with Gary Skoloff of the American Bar Association that the better arrangement is to have one custodial parent with good visitation rights for the other parent.

One observer has likened joint-custody agreements to an old nursery tale: "When they are good, they are very, very good, and when they are bad, they are horrid." Every lawyer I have spoken with could point to a few examples in their experience of very good joint-custody situations. These usually involve one or more of the following factors: parents who have remarried and are happy in their new lives; enough money for the father to buy a house nearby; children who are old enough to ride their bikes back and forth between homes; children who have the same friends in what is basically the same neighborhood; and, most important, a spirit of cooperation among all family members. More often, however, lawyers tell horror stories—of children endlessly delivering hostile messages back and forth between their parents, or of court orders for joint custody that seem preposterous, as in the case of a ten-month-old baby whose parents argue at the slightest contact.

The bitter custody disputes that are splattered across the tabloids also involve ordinary people. Sometimes in court I see a forlorn child being shepherded in or out by a harried parent. I often think that whatever the custody decision, that child will be scarred for life. No child can come through such a harrowing experience as a custody battle without having deep wounds as a result of being evaluated by at least one psychologist and/or psychiatrist, questioned by a judge, told what to say by both parents, and put in a totally untenable position. Issues of loyalty and guilt will plague this child for life.

. . . .

Psychiatrist Richard A. Gardner, who has written many books about divorce, says, "Of all the forms of litigation, custody litigation may very well be the most vicious. After all, the stakes are the highest: involved are one's most treasured possessions, one's children." Dr. Gardner rails against lawyers who exploit their vulnerable clients for the sake of high fees, judges he has encountered who are "uninterested, lazy and uncommitted," and faults the judicial system for even allowing custody matters to be brought into litigation. He believes that the "adversary system is perhaps the worst conceivable method for resolving a child-custody dispute."

Mediation

Dr. Gardner and many others wish to see a program of mandatory mediation for all custody disputes. Some states, such as California, already have this program. Mediation is a process that involves working with a trained professional—a mediator—to resolve conflicts. In matters of divorce, mediation can help settle questions of custody, child support, and property. Mediation is not an adversarial process; that is, the spirit is one of compromise, conciliation, and cooperation.

After all I have written about warring couples, you might naturally ask, "If couples cannot be civil with each other, how in the world can they sit down in the same room to work things out?"

They cannot. Mediation is not suitable for all divorcing couples. They must be ready for it, asserted Isolina Ricci, Ph.D., Director of the Office of Family Court Services for the Administrative Office of the Courts in California in *Family and Conciliation Courts Review*:

It is neither reasonable nor productive to expect a highly dysfunctional or conflicted couple to magically, in a single three-hour mediation session, become fully functional, reasonable, evenly-matched, and capable of honoring agreements. Such families need far more than mediation.

For neutral or friendly couples who can use the services of mediation, the process is structured, the agenda is set at the beginning of the sessions, and it is a good deal less expensive than hiring two lawyers to fight it out. The focus is on problem-solving with a balanced view, so that everyone's needs get taken into consideration.

Hugh McIsaac, director of Family Court Services for Conciliation Court, the mediation unit of Los Angeles County Superior Court, sees mediation as a process of "setting goals for the family, confronting fears each parent may have about the other's actions, and hammering out a compromise that has good things in it for the parents as well as for the children." We are even careful about the words we use, so as not to enflame people," says Patricia Bogin Wisch, Ed.D., a psychologist and Director of Mediation Services of Philadelphia. "Custody, visitation, and child support are not part of our vocabulary," says Wisch. "Children's residence, access to the children, and a transfer of funds are the terms we prefer to use." Wisch feels that it is important to do whatever she can to de-escalate tension and foster the concept of working together.

Very often people come to mediation with a parenting plan already decided. What is not so clear, however, are hidden agendas of individual parents. For example, a father might want to have the children half the time so he won't have to pay child support. And it is almost always a shock when couples look at finances realistically. The amount of money that took care of one household cannot take care of two. Accommodations must be made. How can expenses be decreased? How can income be increased? It is a problem for both members of the couple to solve.

Mediation is not therapy. Since it will only move forward if a couple's anger and bitterness is put aside, a couple may be referred for therapy. In addition, a couple might need other services to help them learn to resolve their disputes.

Most mediators agree that mediation is not a suitable way to resolve disputes when there has been abuse in the family. Experts point out that many battered women are unable or unwilling to speak out about the abuse they have experienced, so mediation becomes one more vehicle for the offender to exercise control. Sheila James Kuehl, an attorney at the Southern California Women's Law Center, believes that men are generally more forceful and dominant in the mediation process, while women have been trained to compromise. The result is that often women are forced to accept an agreement they really do not want. "Where there has been violence in the relationship," says Kuehl, "no agreement can safely be thought of as uncoerced."

Because joint-custody agreements often result from a mediated dispute, women's advocates feel that abused women should not participate in mediation because an abused woman and her children are then put in the position of having to deal with a person with whom they do not want continuing contact, and in fact need protection from. "Battering does not end with divorce or separation; violence often increases when an abusive husband realizes he is losing control over his victim," says Marla Hollandsworth, the Legal Advocate of the House of Ruth, a comprehensive crisis shelter program for battered spouses and their children in Baltimore, Maryland. "Thus joint custody, which forces a continued relationship between the parents, may present an ever-present life-threatening situation for the abused wife." Ricci believes that "the presence of some form of abuse should be a 'stop-sign' to mediation." [Ricci, 1989]

It is generally agreed that the use of mediation has dramatically increased the number of joint-custody agreements. Mediators are not a unified group, and the profession is still relatively new, but many favor joint custody if both husband and wife are considered good parents.

. . . .

Are you willing to mediate? Dr. Sheila Kessler, founder of the Mediation Service of Georgia State University, compiled the following list of questions to ask prospective clients:

1. Is the issue (for example, custody of our children) negotiable?
2. Am I willing to make some compromises?
3. Do I trust my former spouse enough to think he/she will be able to uphold a mutually satisfactory agreement regarding the children? (There is almost always a slight element of doubt.)
4. Am I willing to put aside my anger for a while so that I can deal with the issues (regarding the children) in a rational manner?
5. Can I make a commitment to live up to what I agree to (regarding the children)?
6. Am I capable of listening to the other person's side of the story?
7. Do I see this process (of mediation) in terms of compromise rather than of winning or losing?

You are a good candidate for mediation, rather than litigation, if your answers are mostly "Yes." (For information on how to find a mediator, see page 193.) If successful, mediation will most certainly save you time and money and can help set a cooperative tone for your postdivorce family life.

How the Courts Decide Custody

Rather than use mediation, most divorcing couples will use the traditional legal system. Like the vast majority of professionals in mental-health fields, members of the legal profession have resisted the idea of co-parenting. Lawyers and judges are influenced by the social climate which, for the last 50 years or so, has supported the practice of awarding custody to mothers. "The word custody is a double-edged sword," says Paul Bohannan.

"It means responsibility for the care of somebody. It also means imprisonment."

Now, however, more and more divorced mothers work outside the home, and more and more fathers are claiming their legal right to custody of their children. While Deborah Luepnitz, Phyllis Chesler, and others voice concern that unfit fathers are using the banner of the "new father," along with their superior financial position, to win custody of their children, studies have confirmed that men also can be nurturers and caretakers of the young.

By the late 1970s, joint custody was being recognized as a legal entity. As of January 1978, *Newsweek* reported: "Fifteen states have passed parental-equalizing statutes holding that both parents are to be judged on an equal basis in determining the custody of the child." *Women in Transition: A Feminist Handbook on Separation and Divorce*, written in 1975, states:

> The present trend seems to be away from assuming that either party has a *right* to custody and toward looking at the total family situation and figuring out what would be best for the children. Some courts are trying to develop some guidelines for how this decision is made while in others it depends entirely on the feelings and prejudices of a single judge.

Indeed, the latter has proven true: one judge in Philadelphia is known as the "joint-custody judge," while others are known for their staunch opposition to joint custody and make it very difficult for a couple who wish to share custody of their children.

Many lawyers, like other professionals, are struggling to find ways to help their clients create successful parenting plans after divorce. The simplest scenario is when one parent has always been more involved. Usually, couples tend to continue that arrangement. It is more difficult for lawyers and judges when both parents are actively involved in the child's life. In those cases, says domestic-relations attorney Elaine Smith of Philadelphia, a court battle becomes ridiculous. "The judges go groping in the dark: the father has a barbecue in the backyard, the mother has a swing." This kind of information should not have any relevance to determining custody, but it is often brought into court.

Smith says she has seen many cases in which the parents are fairly compatible, have been evaluated by psychologists and psychiatrists, and know "how to do the dance. They go to PTA meetings, and they really are both fine parents." She and other lawyers have difficulty extracting a parenting arrangement from a psychological evaluation. Professional evaluations, talks with children in the judge's chamber, all conducted supposedly to protect children, only serve to evoke fear and confusion in those same children. Child advocacy programs are now developing in which lawyers and psychologists represent the child in court.

Most lawyers believe that it is best to keep custody decisions out of court. Courts are the arena of last resort; only when parents and their lawyers cannot arrive at a mutually satisfying custody arrangement will the court impose a solution. On the other hand, some parents report that before going to their lawyers they had already agreed on joint custody, only to find that their lawyers were not willing to go along with this agreement.

Marcia Holly, in a *Ms.* magazine article, states:

> *My former husband and I waged a more difficult battle with the lawyers than we did with one another; they wanted one or the other parent named as custodian. We were more fortunate with the representative from Family Services who recommended that our daughter reside with me but that we be given joint custody.*

Lawyers are trained in the adversarial process—that is, one person is right and one person is wrong. Therefore, it can be difficult to find a lawyer who is both competent in family law and sensitive to the emotional needs of families experiencing divorce. Many parents tell distressing stories about going into a lawyer's office wanting to work out a fair parenting and property agreement, only to be forced into using scare tactics and deceit toward the other parent. The spirit of cooperation and compromise disappeared—as did a tremendous amount of money that went to pay lawyer's fees.

"You need to find an attorney who gives you the mixture of support, guidance, information, and even confrontation that works for you," says psychologist Adler. A good lawyer is one who will help you keep the focus of custody negotiations on what is best for your children instead of fomenting anger toward your ex-spouse.

In looking for a lawyer, ask for recommendations from people you trust. Call several lawyers and ask them questions about their practice, their area of expertise, their method of working, and so on. With some good detective work and a little luck you should be able to find a lawyer whose answers inspire your trust and confidence.

Because legal professionals are still struggling with the issues of joint custody, Gary Skoloff feels that court-ordered joint custody, imposed on the parents, is rarely successful. "Invariably," says Skoloff, "the children get killed in it. If we win, the children could lose." He has known some cases in which court-ordered joint custody has worked out, but in most cases the children are caught in a war of logistics that never ends.

Embattled parents who have joint custody of their children often contribute to giving joint custody a bad name. Judges get fed up with parents who continually go back to court to settle minor disputes. "She didn't send back the clothes," or "He let them watch an extra hour of TV" are not issues about which judges enjoy hearing. "When judges see people counting hours and coming back to court to resolve this, they get very angry and then *they* count hours," says attorney Elaine Smith. They might retaliate with an order for a child to spend Christmas Eve with one parent and from 9:00 a.m. to 9:00 p.m. on Christmas Day with the other. "I am shocked that many parents allow a stranger—the judge—to make decisions for them that affect their children's lives. It's really quite sad," says Smith.

Judges are human beings who make decisions based partly on their own experiences, their own family history, their own bias as to who would be a better parent, and other personal reasons. Most judges probably prefer maternal custody, following the nationwide pattern (mothers have primary custody in approximately 90 percent of all cases). Some argue that judges are unduly impressed by a father who shows any interest at all in his children. Even if that interest is newly developed, these judges react favorably and may award custody to a father who is only minimally involved with his children, *especially* if he has more money than the mother (which is likely). Occasionally judges make decisions that are courageous and become landmark cases; conversely, other decisions seem arbitrary and represent the risk of engaging in any custody battle.

Laws about joint custody vary from state to state, although more states have statutes pertaining to joint custody than do not. It's important to remember that in states with joint-custody laws, joint legal custody is usually awarded to both parents, with the mother retaining primary physical custody.

	States with joint-custody statutes†	States that give joint custody preference over other custody arrangements	States that give joint custody preference if both parents request it	States where joint custody cannot be ordered unless both parents agree to it**
Alabama				
Alaska	✔			
Arizona				
Arkansas				
California	✔		✔	
Colorado	✔			
Connecticut	✔			
Delaware	✔			
Florida	✔	✔		
Georgia				
Hawaii	✔			
Idaho	✔	✔		
Illinois	✔			
Indiana	✔			
Iowa	✔	✔		
Kansas	✔	✔		
Kentucky	✔			
Louisiana	✔	✔		
Maine	✔		✔	
Maryland	‡			
Massachusetts	✔	✔		
Michigan	✔			
Minnesota	*			
Mississippi	✔		✔	
Missouri	✔			
Montana	✔	✔		
Nebraska				
Nevada	✔	✔		
New Hampshire	✔	✔		
New Jersey	‡			

(chart continues on next page)

	States with joint-custody statutes†	States that give joint custody preference over other custody arrangements	States that give joint custody preference if both parents request it	States where joint custody cannot be ordered unless both parents agree to it**
New Mexico	✔	✔		
New York				
North Carolina	✔			
North Dakota				
Ohio	✔			✔
Oklahoma	✔			
Oregon	✔			
Pennsylvania	✔			
Rhode Island				
South Carolina				
South Dakota				
Tennessee	✔			
Texas	✔			
Utah	✔	✔		
Vermont	✔		✔	✔
Virginia				
Washington				
West Virginia				
Wisconsin	✔			
Wyoming				
Total	34	12	4	2

Sources: Family Law Quarterly, winter 1988; Jeff Atkinson, Modern Child Custody Practice (1988 supplement); National Conference of State Legislatures.

† No state prohibits joint custody when both parents request it.

‡ No statute; case law only.

* For joint legal custody only. Case law provides primary caretaker presumption for physical custody.

** In states without a statute, case law may require parental agreement.

California has been a leader in establishing joint-custody law. "In 1979," writes attorney Jay Folberg in the *Journal of Family Law*, "California set the trend for a second generation of joint-custody legislation by establishing a legislative preference for joint custody and a presumption that joint custody is in the best interests of children when parents are in agreement." Other states followed California's lead but went even further, maintaining that joint custody would be considered the best option even if the parents did not agree. This concept ended up being incorporated in the interpretation of California law, because its goal was "frequent and continuing contact with both parents."

Later, after a bitter political battle, California amended its law to state that there is neither a preference nor a presumption for or against joint custody unless both parents agree to it. California also has a provision called the "friendly parent" clause, which states that if sole custody is to be granted, the court is obliged to consider which parent is more likely to allow the child or children frequent and continuing contact with the non-custodial parent. [Glazer, 1989] Some argue that this clause makes a mother who is fighting for sole custody appear the less cooperative parent and in turn makes her less likely to win custody.

Guidelines for Choosing Joint Custody

Some states make a distinction between joint legal custody—in which decisions about the health, education, and welfare of the children are shared—to joint physical custody, in which the residence of the children is divided between the mother's and father's homes. In New Jersey, the Supreme Court listed criteria for awarding joint legal custody and joint physical custody. Its criteria used to decide joint legal custody are:

1) the child's relationship with both parents
2) the "fitness" of both parents
3) the parents' willingness to care for the child

4) the parents' ability to separate their personal conflicts from their parenting roles

5) minimal parental cooperation, as assessed by past patterns and not during the "emotional heat" of the divorce

6) the preference of the child, if the child is of "sufficient age and capacity"

The New Jersey Supreme Court went on to list "practical considerations" in awarding joint physical custody:

1) the financial status of the parents
2) the proximity of their homes
3) the demands of parental employment
4) the age and number of children.

[Folberg, 1984–85]

If you were a judge using these criteria, would you award joint legal and/or physical custody to your own family?

Lawyers, judges, politicians, mediators, counselors, mothers, and fathers are realizing that joint custody does not work for everybody. Accordingly, there is a trend to reverse the innovative approach of a few years ago. New Jersey lawyer Skoloff says, "States were saying that to save the children, we had to give them both parents. It sounds terrific. The only problem is that most of the time, it doesn't work out." Some states, such as Colorado, have ruled that joint custody has to be proven beneficial to the child before it is ordered. In some states, a parental plan for implementation of joint custody is required before a ruling about custody is given. Other states do not finalize a joint-custody decision until after a period of time in which the plan can be modified if it is not working.

West Virginia and Minnesota have adopted a "primary caretaker" preference. This means that a judge has to decide which parent is the primary caretaker and award custody to that parent. The court of West Virginia has clearly defined the tasks of the primary caretaker as

1) preparing and planning meals
2) bathing, grooming, and dressing
3) purchasing, cleaning, and care of clothes
4) obtaining medical care, including nursing and trips to physician
5) arranging for social interactions among peers after school, including transporting to friends' houses or, for example, to scout meetings
6) arranging alternative care such as babysitting or day care
7) putting the child to bed at night, attending to the child in the middle of the night, waking the child in the morning
8) disciplining, toilet training, and teaching general manners
9) educating, including religious and cultural education
10) teaching elementary skills such as reading, writing, and arithmetic.

In most families this person is clearly the mother. Those who favor the "primary caretaker" preference feel that since both parents know at the time of divorce who the primary caretaker is, there is much less likelihood of a long court battle for custody.

Federal laws also exist relating to custody. The Uniform Child Custody Jurisdiction Act (UCCJA) and the Parental Kidnapping Prevention Act (PKPA) were enacted to resolve interstate custody disputes and to discourage kidnapping by parents. This means that a joint-custody order from one state will be honored by another state.

"Family law has become a political arena or battleground," says Martha L. Fineman, a professor of law at the University of Wisconsin Law School. She believes that fathers' rights groups have "emerged as a political force." [Glazer, 1989] While joint-custody legislation implies that each parent has equal *rights*, in

· · · · · · · · · ·

practice *responsibilities* are not shared between parents. Yet both parents need to share in their children's upbringing, and, says Jeff Atkinson, a Chicago attorney and author of *Modern Child Custody Practice*, "The benefits of joint custody—for children and parents—should not be blocked by giving one parent veto power over the custody arrangement." [Glazer, 1989]

Two Sample Agreements

How should you go about creating a custody agreement, or if you prefer the term, parenting plan? I will tell you about the separation agreement my ex-husband and I wrote together many years ago. Your relationship with your own ex-spouse may not be one of basic trust and mutual understanding, as ours was. However, I know of many couples who, while not on friendly terms, did agree that they both wanted to be involved with their children and were able to agree rather easily on custody. They just knew they could not fight over the children, and would not consider going to court to settle these matters. If you and your ex-spouse can come to some understanding, the process of mediation, should you choose to use it, will be that much quicker. An agreement that you both work on together is stronger, much more likely to be respected and adhered to, and more likely to suit your family's needs.

The agreement that Jeff and I have lived by is the separation agreement that we wrote. This agreement is not presented here as a document to be reproduced. Our lawyer counseled us that any contract between two individuals is a legal contract; however, unlike other legal contracts, settlements concerned with child support, visitation, and custody are not necessarily final. If our circumstances had changed and one of us wanted to bring a matter into court, it is not clear whether a court would enforce our agreement. This would be true whether an attorney had written the agreement or whether we had written it ourselves. As our attorney stated, "This is a sample and of course the best interest of the child is always paramount and can alter any private agreement or court order as to the child."

. . . .

Jeff and I wrote the first version of our agreement within weeks after we separated, agreed to renegotiate the following year, and then drew up a third version, which remained in effect until Josh moved to Vermont with his father years later. By then, we no longer had a written agreement but we continued to consider ourselves as joint partners in parenting. Very little had changed in the three versions of our agreement.

When we first decided to divorce, we showed our agreement to a lawyer. She suggested that we add Items 6 and 7. Item 6 made sense to each of us: if Jeff should remarry and want to name his new wife as his beneficiary, I would no longer have insurance on Jeff's life. Therefore, I assumed ownership of Jeff's life-insurance policy, and I paid the premiums. That way, I would always have some security as long as I decided to make the payments, and if Jeff wanted to get additional insurance to protect a new wife, he could do that. He, in turn, continued to pay the premiums on my life insurance.

Our lawyer also suggested that we agree on having the right to see each other's paychecks. Jeff and I felt that this was not necessary, since by then we had been trusting each other and dealing in good faith for two years. But the lawyer advised that we protect ourselves on the grounds that one never knows what the future might bring—animosity, other relationships, added financial responsibility, and so on. We agreed, but in the 16 years we have lived apart, we have never asked the other to verify income.

An explanation is necessary about Item 4. Jeff and I each had professions, although at various times we talked about not working at them for a while. At one time I chose not to work at my profession, and I saw this as a luxury on my part. Since I might have been able to increase my income, there was no reason for Jeff to assume more financial responsibility for Josh's costs—and every reason for me to assume a basic level of care for him, no matter what my earnings. I was prepared, too, to support any similar decision Jeff might make: if he had decided not to work for a while, he would still have had to pay 30 percent of Josh's costs, even if his earnings were considerably less.

. . . .

This agreement was written in 1976, and while it may seem naive and simplistic now, it reflects the spirit of the times, the spirit of my relationship with Jeff, and our commitment to co-parenting.

Financial and Custody Agreement For Miriam and Jeffry Galper

Custody of Joshua

We agree that we will have joint custody of Joshua. Who he lives with at what times will be jointly determined by us as we see fit. This includes vacation times, holidays, regular weekly schedule, and summers.

Financial agreement

1. There will be no support paid by either person to the other. Joshua's costs will be arranged for in the following manner: Each of us will pay Joshua's costs, as they arise, for his food, shelter, entertainment, daily transportation, vacations taken with each of us, and any other regular costs that come up when he is living with that parent.

2. Other costs for Joshua, as listed, will be paid for by both of us in ratio to our base earnings (see below). These are:

(a) Doctors (including dental, medical, medicines, hospitalization, Joshua's medical insurance)
(b) Joshua's afterschool babysitter
(c) Joshua's camp, special trips
(d) school, tutorials, other lessons
(e) clothes
(f) big toys (bikes, etc.)
(g) college
(h) allowance

We will each keep a record of our expenses on these items and share them with each other to arrive at who owes what to whom each month, within the first five days of the business month.

3. Our base earnings mean the basic earnings each has on his/her job. This does not include extra earnings from one-shot consultations, book royalties, extra research jobs, and so on. We realize that this could be confusing if one or both of us makes a living from a combination of these odds and ends, but we will try to agree fairly and with goodwill what constitutes our regular earnings and what constitutes extras.

4. If either of us earns so little that he/she would have to pay less than 30 percent of Joshua's costs, she/he has to pay that 30 percent anyway.

5. At whatever point we sell our stocks, bonds, mutual stocks, we split the proceeds equally.

6. We agree to take control and payment of the other person's life insurance.

7. Each of us has the right to see the other's paycheck upon request.

Dated: September, 1976

Signed:

Jeffry Galper_____

Miriam Galper_____

Witnessed:_____

. . . .

It was not difficult to come to this agreement. Jeff and I shared the philosophy that we would each take care of Joshua, emotionally and financially.

Legally, I had custody of Joshua. This was necessary in order for Jeff and me to be granted a divorce in the conservative county where we lived. Although I was Joshua's legal custodian, Jeff and I saw it differently, as the first sentence of our agreement indicates. Years later, it seemed ironic that I had custody of my son, yet he was living 400 miles away with his father. So much for legalities!

Below is a copy of another separation agreement, written by a couple with the help of an attorney. Two especially interesting points are Item 3, which states the age when the children can decide where they will live, and Item 4, which provides a method to settle disputes.

Preliminary Draft

An AGREEMENT OF SEPARATION
Between Alice and Bertrand Jarry

I. Custody of David and Peter to be Shared

1. Bertrand to have the children for four (4) days and five (5) nights each week, specifically, Sunday through Wednesday days and Saturday through Wednesday nights; Alice to have the children the remaining three (3) days and two (2) nights.

Except that, once a month, for one week mutually agreed on from time to time, Alice will have the children for five (5) days and four (4) nights, specifically, Monday through Friday days and Monday through Thursday nights; Bertrand to have the children on such weeks for the remaining two (2) days and three (3) nights.

2. This specification of shared custody is not to be understood as preventing Alice and Bertrand from entering into mutual

. . . .

agreements for either parent to have the children for longer periods of time, such as vacations.

3. The children are not to be separated from each other for periods of longer than two (2) weeks, unless mutually agreed upon by Alice and Bertrand prior to any actual separation of the children from each other.

II. Support of the Children

1. Each parent will be responsible individually for the financial support of the children during the times in which he or she has custody.

2. The parents will be jointly responsible for providing the clothing and medical needs of the children.

3. Bertrand will not be responsible for the support of Alice.

III. Children Not Bound by Agreement After Age 15

Each child may decide for himself, without regard to Parts I and II of this agreement, with whom he will live when he is fifteen (15) years of age.

IV. Intellectual and Spiritual Welfare of the Children

1. The education of both children will be at institutions mutually agreed on by both parents. The parents will meet at least four (4) times each year to discuss ways and means of appropriate education.

In the thirty (30)-day period immediately following the sixth anniversary of this agreement the parents will discuss and make a financially secure and binding arrangement for the educational future of the children.

2. Spiritual training: To be considered at any later, mutually agreed-upon, date.

. . . .

V. Disposition of Properties, now held as Tenants by the Entireties

1. The farm which is located in Williamburg Township, Clark County, Missouri, will be maintained as a partnership between Alice and Bertrand, its responsibilities and benefits to be shared equally.

2. The house and property located at 42 Blackberry Drive, St. Louis, Missouri, will be solely owned and managed by Bertrand, who will have the responsibility for its maintenance and mortgage.

VI. Method for Arbitrating Disputes

A council of five (5) persons, all mutually agreed to, will be selected; two (2) persons to be nominated each by Alice and Bertrand, and one person to be jointly nominated. This council will act to settle any dispute in the terms of this agreement upon the request of either Alice or Bertrand, and render a binding decision on it.

VII. Effect of Possible Future Decree of Divorce to be Null

This agreement is made with the understanding that if at any future time there should be made a decree of divorce between Alice and Bertrand, such a decree would have no effect on the intention and actual provisions of this agreement.

(Alice Jarry)_____

(Bertrand Jarry)_____

April 18, 19——

(Witness)_____

Agreements, whether voluntary or court-ordered, are only as good as the people who make them. If you are a person who lives by your word, then what you write down will have meaning and value. If you are a person who likes to see what you can get away with, who tries to manipulate a situation, and who mocks the ideas of cooperation, compromise, and goodwill, then it doesn't matter what you or any judge has written down for you. There will always be some situation in your life which is not covered by the agreement. If your agreement is court-ordered, what will you do then? Go back to your lawyers? And what if they can't come to an agreement? You'll probably end up back in court. You might be able to do that a few times, assuming that you can afford it, but it is unlikely that a judge will think too kindly of your frequent returns.

You are best off to think of your parenting agreement as one which is beneficial for you and your children, and is something you can live with, now and in the future. Of course, you don't know what the future will bring and what changes will be necessary in your schedule. But you can know that whatever happens, your intent is to work out an agreement that provides you and your children with the best possible solution to a difficult situation.

7

Remarriage

When Dad met Heather, it wasn't bad, it was just new.
[Chelsea, age 14]

As if joint custody weren't complicated enough, remarriage creates yet another family, often including more children who have a different set of arrangements and schedules, to say nothing of individual values. It's not just the actual schedule that you must contend with, but also the unwritten norms of "the way we do things." The more people in any family configuration, the more complicated life can be.

Simultaneously, remarriage by one parent evokes strong feelings in the other. When your former spouse remarries, you might relive the pain of the original separation and wonder if you made a mistake in getting a divorce. Even if you also remarried some time ago, you might feel jealous and competitive, and miss your ex-mate. Questions of possible changes in custody arrangements and finances arise. Will someone else be disciplining your children? How will you maintain your role as parent to your children with someone of the same sex now in their lives? It is a time of great uncertainty for both you and your children.

Two Parents, Two Families

Mark Gordon and his former wife Naomi are a model of the binuclear family. The Gordons were once a couple; now each has remarried. They have two distinct households, live next door to one another, and have worked out their joint-custody schedules to coincide.

Naomi and Mark have two daughters, Lauren and Chelsea. After the divorce, Mark married Heather, who had two sons, Paul and Dylan, from a previous marriage. Naomi married Gary, who had not married before and was childless. Together they have one son, Ben. So now, where there was once just one family—two parents and two children—there are now two families, with four parents and five children. Not included for simplicity's sake are Heather's ex-husband, his second wife, his third child, and his second divorce.

When Heather and Mark first became a couple, her sons were with her during the week and every other weekend. Mark's daughters were with him from Sunday noon through Wednesday afternoon. That meant that there were times when Mark was living with Heather and her boys, while his daughters were at their mom's house. This was a difficult experience for Mark. It was strange to be responsible for someone else's children. Moreover, being with Paul and Dylan made him miss his daughters even more. Paul and Dylan were a constant reminder to Mark that his family had split up and that he would not be with his daughters for a few days. This also increased his loneliness and sense of incompletion as a father.

Like all new stepparents, Mark and Heather had to work out their parenting roles. Was it a good idea for Mark to discipline Heather's sons? Heather found herself becoming very defensive and protective when Mark intervened in her parenting. In addition, Heather found herself in the midst of Mark's struggles with Naomi, his ex-wife, to assert himself as a full and equal parent to their daughters. "We had every support such as therapy and counseling and advice from people experienced in these matters, and as much awareness as anyone could have, and still it was difficult," Heather recalls.

It was hard to know where the boundaries stood between the two families, and it was hard for Heather to know when to step back and let Mark work out his own negotiations with Naomi. "It was difficult to know what my place was, what my role was," says Heather.

Heather agreed with Mark to keep the schedule he and Naomi had created for their daughters. "We worked our lives around that schedule," says Heather, "and while it was rigid, it also gave all of us the structure we needed." Mark's schedule with his daughters influenced Heather to ask her ex-husband to spend more time with his sons. As a result, Heather and her ex-husband now have a joint-custody agreement patterned after the one set up by Mark and Naomi. This allows Mark and Heather some child-free days as well as days when all four children are with them. Another benefit is that Paul and Dylan spend a lot more time with their dad.

"Each year was like a hurdle to get over," says Heather. "It has gotten easier, although not without a lot of difficulty and struggle."

One of the most difficult issues to negotiate was holidays—coordinating *where* the four children would be on various holidays and deciding *how* they would spend them. In their early years together, the pain of their divorces would resurface at holidays—for Mark, Heather, and their children. Holidays reminded everyone that their original families were not together, that somehow they weren't like other families, enjoying the events

. . . .

together. Because so much energy was spent just getting through the holidays and dividing the children's time equally, there was no emotional energy left over to have a meaningful holiday together as a blended family.

"In time I realized that the kids had preferences about how they wanted to celebrate holidays, and I didn't have to be the one to create a new tradition all by myself," says Heather.

Naomi and her second husband, Gary, had other concerns. Like Heather, Gary was uncertain about his new role as a stepparent, but he adapted well to the joint-custody routine. However, when Naomi and Gary had a child of their own, things became more complicated. Their son wondered where his big sisters were going on Sundays and why they had to leave him. The concept of divorce and joint custody was confusing for him.

"He still doesn't like it when the girls leave to go to their father's house," says Naomi. "On the other hand, he has gained another family and is close to the girls' father, their stepbrothers Paul and Dylan, and Heather."

In their second marriages, the Gordons have worked hard to make a stable life for their five children, four of whom live in joint-custody arrangements. They plan holiday events and keep the children's best interests in mind. This past Mother's Day, Naomi decided to invite Mark and Heather and her sons over for dinner so that her daughters wouldn't feel conflict about where to celebrate the event. Thus, Naomi got to spend an important day with her three children.

"It's really fun now to have all the children with us," says Heather. "I'm just grateful the years have passed."

Heather estimates that it took three years for their families to smooth out the major difficulties: Naomi and Mark dissolving their spousal relationship while maintaining their parental system; the new spouses, Heather and Gary, figuring out where they belonged in the system; the children moving back and forth between their parents' homes; and little Ben getting accustomed to staying behind when his sisters left for their dad's house. There

. . . .

were many needs to consider, with a lot of conflicting feelings, loyalties, desires, and frustrations. That both families have managed so well testifies to the parents' commitment to the well-being of their children.

Conflict and Competition

Other joint-custody families affected by second marriages have not fared as well. Resentment and jealousy often characterize relations in some families, especially those in which a father has joint custody of his children and a mother has sole custody of hers. For example, Jessica and Scott, now divorced, have a son and a daughter. Two years ago, Scott married Marci, who also has a son and a daughter from a previous marriage. Jessica and Scott share parenting responsibilities for their children, while Marci has sole custody of her children, who see their father from time to time.

Marci resents the fact that Scott's children come and go as if they are honored guests in her home, with certain privileges that her children don't have. They aren't responsible for as many chores as her children. When things aren't going well they can always tell Marci that she's not their mother and to stop telling them what to do. Marci is required to be extraordinarily flexible, accepting the schedule that Jessica and Scott have agreed to for their children even though it affects her life considerably. She wants to have a voice in the arrangements, but Scott believes such arrangements should be handled between Jessica and himself. Marci also thinks that Scott spends far too much time discussing the children with his ex-wife. Why is there so much to talk about? Her children are doing just fine, and she rarely talks to their father about how they're getting along. Perhaps she would like to, but they have not established that kind of relationship.

Marci's own children are jealous of the relationship that Scott has with his children. Their own father is not nearly as attentive to them. They watch with envy as Scott dotes on his children, and, while he is kind to Marci's children, they feel left out when Scott's own children are present. They have to share the bathroom, toys, and even their bedrooms. Before Marci and Scott married, each child had a room. Now, every other week that room is invaded by one of Scott's children. They feel that if Scott had two girls and they were two boys, then they could at least be together by themselves. But instead, they each have to share a room because boys and girls can't share the same room. They feel it's all unfair.

Jessica doesn't think it's fair, either. She has not remarried and is jealous of the cozy life Scott now has with Marci. She envisions that the two of them with the children make one big happy family. She is concerned that her children will decide they want to live a more normal life and stay with their father all the time. She worries that one day they will get tired of moving back and forth. Jessica is convinced that Scott and Marci can offer her children more than she can: more toys, more friends, a bigger television screen, and a mom and a dad, all in one place. Even though she hears stories about the conflicts the children have, Jessica knows it is also fun for them sometimes, and she worries that their desire for a more stable life will outweigh her relationship with them.

Jessica also doesn't like calling her children while they're at their father's house. She doesn't like talking to Marci, and she feels especially foolish when Marci's children answer the phone. She wonders what they think of her, what Scott says about her behind her back, and if her children are loyal to her. Scott ended their marriage to marry Marci, and Jessica thinks she will never feel comfortable in Marci's presence. She wonders what they will do when the children graduate from high school or college or get married, and the three adults have to be in the same place at the same time.

Jessica and Scott's children don't have an easy time, either. They feel that they are competing for Scott's affection—not only with Marci, but with her children as well. They wonder where they fit in, especially since the household they enter every other week seems to go on fine without them. What really happens

· · · · · · · · · ·

when they're away? Does their father buy toys for Marci's children and take them out to dinner? Do Dad and Marci and her kids curl up in front of the television and watch a special show together? Scott's children feel that as much as their father tries to make his home feel like theirs, in one way or another they always feel like outsiders.

"The greater the number of children, the greater the opportunities for jealousy and rivalry for parental affection," say Drs. Emily and John Visher, preeminent authorities on stepfamily life and authors of *How to Win as a Stepfamily*. Scott's children wonder if he will have children with Marci, and then what? Where could they possibly fit in his life? Maybe the house would just be too crowded and they'd live with Jessica full time. They'd miss Scott, but he'd be too busy for them anyway.

Scott might be too busy for them even now, because he is busy trying to please two women—his ex-wife, whom he feels terribly guilty about leaving, and his present wife, who seems angry all the time. No matter what he does, one of them seems unhappy with him.

Are there any solutions to these intricate problems? I have found that some issues are open to negotiations and compromise over time, while other issues may never be resolved to everyone's satisfaction. Marci and Scott have been married for just two years—a very short time to adjust to all the changes in postdivorce life.

Communication and Cooperation

Scott and Marci are the key to the success of this new family. Their relationship will set the tone for how everything is handled—from jealousy and envy on the part of the children to Marci's feelings of exclusion when arrangements are made and Jessica's feelings of betrayal and isolation. If Marci and Scott are unified in their commitment to form a strong new family by sharing their own feelings with each other, listening to their children's concerns, easing pain, and building new traditions, over time their difficulties will lessen.

Marci and Scott need to institute a family meeting, held regularly. They need to listen to their children's complaints and hurts and recognize that this is a hard transition for everyone. Perhaps one of the children has a suggestion for making things easier. A special event planned when Scott's children come back to their house or a time when everyone gathers for a treat of some sort can help bring this family together.

Every member of a stepfamily has expectations about how things will be, and every member of a stepfamily is disappointed when those expectations are not met. Whether the new couple likes it or not, and whether or not there is joint custody, every stepchild is a member, in some way, of two households—not one big happy family. Marci and Scott will be helping their children if they include both families in their lives, either by talking about the other parent, planning to buy a gift for that parent at holiday time, or, if possible, including the parent in some celebration. Children know that they have two parents in two different homes. When a parent or stepparent prefers to act as if one parent doesn't exist, a child's reality can become distorted.

Scott needs to tell his ex-wife, Jessica, that he has every intention of supporting her position as mother of his children, that he will do nothing to exclude her from their lives, and that he will inform her of all important events. Scott should also reassure Jessica that Marci understands and accepts this, and that she will not do anything to undermine Jessica's position as mother to her children.

In time, perhaps Marci and Jessica could have their own relationship. This cannot be imposed in any way, but would benefit everyone in the family. I have known families in which the two women—the biological parent and the stepparent—make all the arrangements concerning the children. They even talk about their common ground—one's ex-husband and the other's present husband.

Ian and Valerie live together. Ian has joint custody of his children and Valerie has no children of her own. Valerie has devoted herself to Ian, taking care of his children when they are with them and taking them places when Ian's work schedule prohibits it. For the most part, Valerie has accepted their life together, but she resents the fact that she and Ian have no weekends alone together (the children are with them from Thursday through Sunday), that their lives revolve around the children, and that she has to compete for Ian's attention. She sometimes feels like a little kid herself. Valerie knows not to say, "Choose me or the kids," because she knows she would lose, but she does want to feel more important to Ian.

This couple, who plan to marry, have yet to put themselves first. Ian's primary concern is for his children. Given the bitter court battle he endured to win joint custody, coupled with his devotion to his children, it's only normal for him to feel that his relationship with his children is the most important thing in his life.

It may take years for a shift in attitude to occur, but unless it does, Valerie and Ian's relationship will always be tense. Unless they view their own relationship as central and focus on their needs as a couple, while creating a safe environment for the children, issues of stepfamily life will always be problematic for them.

In *Mom's House, Dad's House*, Isolina Ricci provides a checklist of issues to consider when one parent remarries. For instance, she says that one should "expect issues of custody, support, and authority to be either discussed or reopened." It may be time to review custody arrangements and reevaluate them. Ricci also suggests that you "reach out and give the other biological parent some reassurances that you want the working relationship to continue." Ricci outlines steps, such as those the Gordons took, to keep the lines of communication open between the biological parents, without interference from the new spouses.

I suggest you take a look at *Mom's House, Dad's House*, as

· · · · · · · · · ·

well as the other excellent books on stepparenting listed in the *Suggested Readings* section at the end of this volume. These books offer helpful suggestions and advice from those who have experience. If after several years you are still struggling with postdivorce relationships in your second family, seek the help of a professional family counselor. In the families I have talked about, each person has his or her own perspective and feelings. People need to be heard. If you as a parent feel unable to listen well, then find someone to guide you and your new mate in working out healthy solutions for yourself and your family.

Don't wait. Begin now.

8

. . . .

Facing the Difficulties

Whether you are married or divorced, conflict in childrearing is unavoidable. The task is to see conflict not as something to be avoided at all costs but as an opportunity for growth.

What can you learn about yourself in this conflict? How was conflict handled in your family when you were a child? Women are most often the peacemakers in families, giving in so as to not upset anyone—and giving up their power as well. Conflict is an opportunity for women to be peacemakers of power, not of passivity. With a commitment to resolving conflict, there is often a deepening of relationships and a greater understanding of ·ourselves and others.

If you and your ex-spouse are in conflict, think about your common goals. What do you want to happen? If you want to see your children adjust well to your divorce, how is this conflict

. . . .

serving that end? If your goal is to help your children feel a sense of stability and ongoing connectedness with both of you, how can you resolve this particular conflict to meet that goal? Think of your higher purpose, one that you and your ex-spouse have in common. This often helps to minimize the conflict by putting it into perspective.

Transition Times

I feel empty inside when my kids are gone. I can't ask them how their day was, I can't help them with their homework, I can't tuck them in at night. It's only three days that they're gone, but I really miss them until they get back. [Jack]

The most obvious difficulty with joint custody is that you are not with your children every day. For most parents in the initial stages of a separation, this is a uniquely painful time. You long for your children, in a way that can only be described as heartache. This empty feeling is especially intense for the parent who is used to doing the primary parenting. If there are no children around to pack lunches for, get off to school in the morning, make dinner for in the evening, and go through bedtime routines with, life can seem meaningless. The change from being an active parent to a person with no children at home is abrupt and very difficult.

Both parents experience the loneliness. When a father moves out of the house, as often happens, he is faced with being totally alone and away from all that is familiar—his wife, his children, his belongings. He knows that the children will be an ongoing part of his life, but on the days they are not with him, he often feels bereft. One father described the feeling as a "stunning silence, the silence of being alone, the silence of being without my children."

Constant separations are a difficult part of joint custody, and there seems to be no way to avoid them. You can, however, prepare yourself and your children for the times you'll be apart. What have you wanted to do that requires some time alone? If you haven't done so before, now is the time to consider your career. Do you desire any special training for your career? Take a class. Begin developing your independent life. An exercise class can be a good diversion. Spend time with friends. Use the time wisely—it might still feel lonely for you, but at least you'll be productive.

Another element of the constant separations is difficult to manage: no sooner have you and the children adjusted to being together again when, a few days later, you find yourself pulling back from them in anticipation of their departure. Or you may notice the children withdrawing from you, which makes you feel terrible, since the time you have together is so short. Talk to the children about your feelings. If you are experiencing the pain of separation, they are as well. Acknowledge the difficulty you and your children are having with the comings and goings. You might say, "This is a hard time for me and I know it must be hard for you. Let's talk about it." You can tell them that as time passes, you hope it will get easier for everyone.

Separations are difficult because they remind you of the pain surrounding your divorce. They also remind you of earlier times in your life when someone left you or otherwise disappointed you. Your feelings of being abandoned, a feeling of loss which everyone experiences at some time, resurfaces at times like these and leaves you feeling quite vulnerable. Some parents have an extremely difficult time when their children are with the other parent. If the other parent lives quite a distance away and your time apart from your child will be longer than a week or two, I suggest you read my book *Long Distance Parenting* for suggestions on how to cope with this kind of separation and loss. I also suggest counseling. You may feel very alone, but there are people who can understand what you are going through and can help ease the pain.

There are times when joint custody as a way of life can seem absolutely crazy, particularly during transition times. Joint-custody parents are constantly adjusting to being with their child again after an absence of a few days, and then saying good-bye for a few more days.

The kids need readjustment time each weekend right after the transition from Lou's home to mine. It seems like I have to lay down the law every week and bang a few heads to make sure that they remember what they can and can't get away with at my house. Sometimes the process can be quite trying. [Gloria]

A typical series of events, familiar to many joint-custody parents, is the following: it is the end of the summer and you have been by yourself; your daughter has been with her other parent for two weeks. Transition time is rapidly approaching and you are eager to see your little girl. At last, with much hugging and kissing, you greet her. Then you and she proceed to have an awful time together for the next two days. You argue and get on each other's nerves, her behavior is obnoxious, and you wonder what in the world you were looking forward to.

Finally, you do ease into being with each other, although after two days of annoyance you can hardly call it easing in. School will be starting in another day, and you spend some good times together getting ready. You buy new clothes, school supplies, a special pad, a new lunchbox; you talk about new teachers and who will be in what class. You feel proud of your little girl entering third grade, and you can hardly believe how quickly the years have gone by. You've forgotten that it has taken a while to adjust to being together again after a two-week absence, and it feels as though the irritations of the last few days have ended. The closeness that you're feeling with your daughter now was worth the hard times of a few days ago.

The opening day of school happens to be a Thursday. Your child has actually taken a bath and washed her hair the night before, looks lovely, and is happy to be the first one at the bus stop. Soon the other children begin to arrive with their parents, and you all wait together, excitedly, for the bus. Finally, your daughter goes off to school. Because it's Thursday—your transition day—you won't see her again until Sunday morning. This seems like an incredibly long time to wait to find out about the opening

. . . .

day of school. Of course, you could call to find out how things went that first day, but it's just not the same as being together that afternoon.

School opens only once a year, but there are many occasions when separation feels particularly poignant and upsetting.

The reverse of this pattern is also difficult. When you are alone with your child for a longer-than-usual time, you really begin to feel like a normal parent. You get to know your child's rhythms and moods very well and have what feels like an exceedingly intimate time together. If feels good to know what it is like to be with your child day in and day out, day after day. The hard part comes when you have to separate.

The first day of the week that I don't have Britt, very often I'll get suddenly depressed, so I'll go visit a friend who has kids and spend some time with them, just to be around kids. I feel as though all of a sudden there is a tremendous loss and change. [Kurt]

Even though the passing of time does make separations easier, most parents do experience a tug in their heart when it's time to say good-bye.

Planning for the Unexpected

Other difficulties for joint-custody families involve scheduling holidays, vacations, and special occasions. While not as weighty an issue as where the children will live, this often is a very emotional issue. Difficulties arise when the unexpected happens. For instance, you have a plan for summer vacations: the children are with each of you for two weeks during the summer, and follow the usual schedule the rest of the time. When your children are older, however, they will want to go away by themselves, perhaps to camp, or on a trip to visit friends. When your son, who has been away from both parents, returns, whose home does he go to?

When your daughter comes home on break from her first semester away at college, where does she sleep that night? These situations can be managed if a spirit of goodwill prevails.

When I first came home from school during my freshman year, I'd follow the regular schedule. Only my dad needed my room for one of my stepbrothers, so I slept on the sofa bed in the living room. The next year, it just sort of happened that I'd sleep at my mom's house when I was home and I'd visit, talk, have dinner at my dad's. The only thing that made me feel torn is when my parents got upset about where I'd slept. But everyone has been very nice about it, really. [Lauren]

Another anxiety-producing time is the end-of-the-year holiday season:

Christmas is really the hardest time for us. Both George and I have always felt tremendous strain about the family being split up at Christmas time. We've always managed to make it okay for the kids, but for us it's the worst time to get through. Do you know that every year we've almost gotten back together again at Christmas? We've talked about it every year and it's almost happened. For the past few years, whichever one of us wasn't living in the house would move back in and stay overnight for Christmas—not just for the day, but through the New Year's holiday.

There's really a strong sense of priority of the family ties, of having the warm hearth around which everyone gathers and the sense of being rooted with these people. Around Christmas all those things begin to seem more important than anything else. Even this year I have found myself thinking about getting back together with George already—thinking, "Why don't we be more realistic and realize that life is not about having these perfect relationships? Life is about raising children, having a stable home, and all those things."

*But then I felt that I wouldn't want to be over there for
Christmas this year. I don't really feel good in that situation. Yes,
we're going to try to split it as we've done on the other holidays,
alternating from year to year. One Thanksgiving the kids are with
one parent, and one Thanksgiving with the other. And we're going
to do that with Christmas, only we're going to try dividing the time
so that each of us gets to spend some of Christmas with the
children. However we do it, I know it will hurt.* [Julia]

Ordinary days that deviate from the routine can present a
problem, too. When your child doesn't have a full day of school,
for whatever reason, how will you handle it? Most parents
coordinate to see who can take care of the child or arrange for
care, either by a friend or babysitter. Some parents who are unable
to work out the smaller details have an understanding that if a
half-day of school falls on a Wednesday, and Wednesday is the
mother's day, then she has to make arrangements. When the school
calls to say that your child is sick and needs to be picked up, who
will do it? You can decide on the basis of who is responsible that
day or who has the more flexible schedule, regardless of whose
official day it is.

These issues in themselves are not difficult to handle. All
parents are constantly making such arrangements. In more
traditional homes, these tasks usually are the mother's. But co-
parenting assumes that both parents will assume responsibility for
the child's day-to-day living. That means a lot of phone calls, and
a lot of checking back and forth. But in this situation you are in
continuous contact with your ex-spouse, maintaining the parent
system while working to dissolve the spouse system. It can be
difficult emotionally to talk to someone so often when your
feelings toward that person may be, at best, unresolved.

These frequent phone calls and arrangements are most
difficult in the beginning of a separation. At this point you haven't
yet worked out your new co-parenting style. One of you may
prefer a lot of contact, while the other prefers privacy. It can also

lead to hurt feelings and wondering if this joint-custody business is going to work out for you at all. In time, however, it is likely that this situation will get easier for you. But this is one of the most difficult aspects of joint custody—letting your ex-spouse know what's going on when your child is with you, sharing important information, planning and arranging. It seems endless, and it is.

Early on, it was thought that joint custody would force warring parents to cooperate. That doesn't always prove to be true. Researcher William Coysch and his colleagues at the Center for the Family in Transition in Corte Madera, California, found that custody did not determine how parents would relate to each other. In fact, the better predictor of how parents would relate to each other after divorce was their emotional adjustment before the divorce.

For many parents it becomes routine to call the ex-spouse and make the appropriate arrangements regarding the children. This can become a simple businesslike operation in which the tone is either friendly or neutral. Of course, it takes time to achieve this level of communication and trust.

As children get older, other sensitive issues may develop. Adolescents usually don't choose to spend a lot of time with their parents. What happens to a teenage boy whose parents pressure him to spend time with each of them? He may find this situation unbearable. He may not want to leave one parent's home for that of the other, especially as a weekend of social events comes up. What happens then to the schedule and the principle of equal time? For the sake of family harmony and a teenager's needs, principles may have to be reconsidered.

It's difficult to envision co-parenting working as smoothly for an older child as for a younger one, yet I know many families whose schedule has continued through high school. Since we really have no idea what the future will bring, it is not time well spent to worry about how things will work out five or ten years from now. In many cases, however, as children get older and the marital status of divorced parents changes, the need to alter

. . . .

custody arrangements becomes more prevalent. "Children are not frozen at the age of the initial custody decision," says W. Glenn Clingempeel of Temple University ". . .and the type of custody may need to change as the preferences and needs of the child change." If your relationship with your ex-spouse is cooperative and you maintain an attitude of openness and flexibility, you will be able to create new arrangements to suit your children's changing needs.

Moving

The very word—"moving"—sends shivers down a joint-custody parent's spine. A flood of anxious questions come to mind: if one parent wants to move, what happens? Who has the children for the school year and who has them for vacations? Does it still feel like joint custody? And what if you know you need or want to move and want to take the children with you, but your ex-spouse wants them to stay? Does a major custody fight ensue? How on earth do you decide what to do?

Many couples decide to stay put. Says Barbara:

I don't think about moving. I'll be here until my son goes off to college and so will my ex-husband. It's important enough to me that both of us are here to parent our son that I would not leave the area. I'm not talking about my entire life, but a period in it. When my son is ready for college, I'll be only 44. That seems real young to me now.

This is not a sacrificial attitude on Barbara's part. She feels that it is in her best interest, as well as her son's, for her to stay put—even though she knows that some couples do manage effective joint custody over long distances.

Soon after I separated from my husband Jeff, he was offered a job in Ottawa. In what now seems like a moment of temporary insanity, we talked about what it would mean for us both to move there, taking up separate residences. It quickly seemed an absurd solution, one that would cause even greater problems, since we would be thrown together and be away from our friends, at a time when we were still separating from each other emotionally. This job offer gave both of us the opportunity to see how difficult it would be for one or both of us to move.

Four years after we separated, Jeff and I both began considering moving to another part of the local area. This posed some difficult questions. Should we work toward moving as close together as possible, for continued ease in shared parenting? That would mean that we would probably run into each other much more. Or should we try to move into separate neighborhoods for the sake of more geographical, and therefore more emotional, distance between us, even if it would mean more disruptions? If we lived some distance apart, how would Josh's boots get from one house to the other on the first snowy morning of the season? Should we even discuss it, or should each of us do what we wanted without planning it all out? And how would such a move affect Josh?

As it turned out, we moved two blocks away from each other and found new ease in our joint-custody life. Josh was able to go from one house to the other by himself. If he left something he wanted at my house, he could easily get it himself. He walked past my house on the way to school every morning, so we had extra chances for hugs and kisses. Our schedule, while we kept to its basic format, seemed much less rigid. Living close by meant that Josh's friends were all in the same neighborhood. Life seemed a lot easier to manage.

My friend Charlotte was not at all sure that she wanted to continue living in the same city where her daughter and her daughter's father lived. Thirteen years ago, she thought she would probably move away from that city. Jim, her ex-husband, said he would never move, because his new wife wanted to stay near *her* ex-husband and their son. Charlotte always assumed that if she moved, her daughter Julie would stay with Jim and his new wife.

Years went by. Charlotte never moved, and she and Julie became very close. Now Julie lives with her mother three weeks out of every four.

Of course, some joint-custody parents do move. My son's father was one of them. After ten years of very cooperative and successful joint custody, Jeff decided he wanted to move to Vermont. Josh was 14 and about to enter high school. I had remarried and become stepmother to a nine-year-old girl.

Jeff and I had intense discussions about where Josh would live. He could stay with me and adjust to a new stepfather (whom he affectionately referred to as his "fake father") and an alien child (*yucch!* a *girl!*), or he could move to Vermont with Jeff. To complicate matters, my husband and I were thinking about moving to California. Josh said that if I were to move to California and Jeff to Vermont, we would have to decide for him where he would live. Eventually I decided to stay in Philadelphia, and Josh opted for Vermont, his dad, and adventure.

His decision made sense to me. He was a boy just coming of age, and he wanted to be close to his father, who could teach him how to be a man in the world. Staying in Philadelphia was not appealing, since he would have to share his mother with a stepfather and a stepsister.

Some would argue that the decision should not have been Josh's to make, no matter what the circumstances—that any child who has to choose one parent over the other is caught in the middle and will suffer intense loyalty conflicts. That is true if the parents are both tugging at a child to choose them, especially in the heat of a court battle. However, Jeff and I both felt secure enough in our relationship with Josh to know that our love and support would transcend miles, no matter where Josh lived.

Legally, I had sole custody. Of course, Jeff and I never took that literally. But here I was, ten years later, the parent with custody, living without my son. It was a very difficult time for me, adjusting to living without daily contact with him, being 400 miles apart.

There is always a possibility that you or your ex-spouse will want to move. A new love, a new job, a new adventure—who knows what the reason will be? A move is an upheaval in every family member's life—for you, your ex-spouse, your children. It is possible to live through it and continue to have meaningful relationships with your children, but I don't recommend a move. If you can avoid moving away from your children, avoid it. If you are moving and assume that you will take the children with you, consider how your move will affect their relationship with their other parent. Long-distance parenting is the least preferable custody choice. In some states, joint-custody decrees imposed by the court often restrict long-distance moves with the child. At the very least joint decision-making will be more difficult, and frequent contact with both parents impossible.

The best decision, as in all matters pertaining to children, is one that parents agree to, not one imposed by a judge. If one of you is considering a move, evaluate carefully. Talk with your ex-spouse to see if you can come up with a list of options. Perhaps your younger son will remain where he is, but when he is ready for high school, he'll move to live with the other parent. Of course, you risk your child deciding, at that point, that he is opposed to such a plan. Do you tell him that he has no choice? Yes, you do, if as his parents you believe it's in his best interests to move, you have agreed on it, and you don't want him to have a choice in the matter. But if a teenager voices a strong preference, most parents will let a child choose where to live. It is difficult enough living with an adolescent, not to mention one who feels he is being held captive.

I worry that when Rianna reaches puberty she'll decide to live with her father. That's a tense time anyway between mother and daughter, and a time when kids look at things through different eyes. Her father has a big house and a lot more money than I have. When she gets to be a teenager she may be more attracted to that way of life. My concern is that I don't think joint custody is a thing that's going to last forever. [Susan]

. . . .

Susan is right. Joint custody will not last forever, perhaps not even until your children finish high school and move away from home. In many families joint custody lasts for a time after parents separate, and then another family form evolves. Your daughter, the older child, might decide that after a number of years, the two-home system isn't working for her any longer.

If your younger child is still content to switch homes weekly, what should you do? How can you meet the needs of each child and still maintain some sense of family? Many families have worked out schedules which, while confusing to an outsider, work well for them. For example, one teen lives with one parent exclusively and visits her other parent and her younger brother regularly. Her brother still moves back and forth between homes.

Split custody arrangements—in which one child lives with one parent and another child with the other parent—are not unusual, especially when there are long distances between homes. Is split custody a good idea for your family? Once again, it depends. It depends on the ages of your children, whether they have spent enough time together under one roof to have a strong sense of kinship, whether they have resolved their sibling rivalry, and whether they would feel abandoned by one parent. Split custody may be the best solution for your family, but it is a decision that has long-lasting consequences, so it should be considered very seriously.

New Relationships

Many co-parents report that some of the most awkward and troublesome situations occur when they begin to form loving relationships with other adults. Their children seem extremely threatened and jealous, and their new mates have difficulty adjusting to the fact that their partners have an intimate relationship with their children. It seems that everyone has strong feelings, and the co-parent feels caught in the middle. All separated and divorced parents have to work out these new relationships, but compared with a parent in a primary role, the co-parent has more day-to-day time away from the children in which to pursue other relationships.

My children have never had to deal with my having another man around. My social involvements with men have always been on my own time, and I never even had a significant relationship where I'd want to bring a man home to the kids. Now, all of a sudden, there's this big guy around and the children are upset. And the big guy, Dick, he's upset too. He's not used to being around kids and I don't think he understands very well how they work. And then there's me. I guess it's all worth it, but sometimes I wonder. [Julia]

Another parent, Jim, points out:

We don't even have words to identify the relationships our children have with significant adults in their lives who are not their parents.

I'm Julie's father and Charlotte is her mother. That's safe and established. But Julie really didn't know what to call Anne, the woman I married, and Kyle, her son. Anne is definitely not her mother but is clearly a significant person in her life. She made up the name of the "Da Family." Anne is her Da Mom and Kyle is her Da brother. It seems to work for her.

What happens if you form a relationship with a man who wants to be an active parent to your son? Your child already has two active parents. It's not as if his father sees him only occasionally or is minimally involved in childrearing, so that someone else could easily fill that role. If you decide to live with this new man, you will have to integrate him into your relationship with your child and also into your relationship with your ex-spouse, since both relationships are structured around co-parenting.

· · · · · · · · · ·

There's a new man in my life and he wants to be part of my family. He wants to be a father to my daughter, Judy, and I don't know how that's going to affect my relationship with my ex-husband and Judy's relationship with her father. Judy is feeling a lot of conflict already. Jonathan is a warm, loving person and while Judy's father is very involved with her, he's just not demonstrative at all. So if she likes Jonathan, is she being disloyal to her father? We've talked abut how she can get different things from different people, but I just don't know how it will all work out. [Nancy]

How is your relationship with your ex-spouse affected if this new man has no children of his own and wants the responsibilities of a parent in relation to your child? Will the three of you go to parent-teacher conferences? How would that feel to all of you? This might best be decided in a three-way discussion. Would you all feel comfortable being at the child's birthday party or graduation? All parents and surrogate parents will want to be part of these events, but for some parents the presence of an ex-spouse's new mate at a celebration is difficult at best.

These are sensitive situations that need to be worked out thoughtfully. Put yourself in the other person's shoes. It is never easy to see your ex-spouse with a new love, even if years have gone by, even if you have remarried. It is painful to know that someone has taken your place. And your children know it, too.

Ideally there should be room for lots of loving adults in a child's life, and some adults and children are better able to handle this than others. Time is a great healer. What may feel impossible and unworkable to you six months after the separation can feel very different three to five years down the road.

What Will People Think?

Wondering how your arrangement will work out and how it will affect your children in the future is one of the costs of doing something for which there are no time-honored rules. One book

says that your child needs one home, not two; another book says
that two homes are better than one. Another book, this one, says
that it depends. You and your ex-spouse are the experts about your
children. If you agree on a parenting plan and if you don't fight,
your children, for the most part, will be fine. If you disagree,
have to go to court, and continue arguing through the years,
it doesn't matter how many homes your children have. They
will have problems.

What is most important to me is that both of us have a primary
role in parenting Luke. Yes, we've had our struggles, but I have to
keep in mind the advantage to Luke and then I act accordingly. He
has an active, healthy relationship with both his parents. Neither
has abandoned him. [Russell]

When you decide to co-parent, you agree to pursue what is
still often seen as an unconventional arrangement. You not only
have to face your own anxiety and doubts about the soundness of
your parenting arrangement, but also those of your family, friends,
and community. Although joint custody is more common today,
many people will question your plan for caring for your children
and will tell you stories of similar arrangements that have not
worked for other families. Although you may not ask for the
opinions of others, you will hear them all the same.

Questions and comments like these are heard often from
people who are skeptical about joint-custody arrangements:
    —"That must be very hard on your child. She must be
      very confused."
    —"Don't you miss him on the days that you don't see him?"
    —"A child needs one home, not two."
    —"How does she know where she's supposed to be?"

It is hard to respond to such comments. You have enough of
your own concerns, and don't especially feel like listening to other
people's worries about your children. One woman I know is often
asked how in the world her seven-year-old son could possibly

keep straight the arrangement she and her ex-husband have worked out. "He just knows, that's all," is her answer. Her seven-year-old, also named Joshua, has never had any trouble remembering where he is supposed to be on any day of the week. Still, the concept of co-parenting is not easy for many adults to accept.

You may find that your children's teachers are reluctant to accept your joint-custody arrangement. We were the only joint-custody family in our community when Josh was young. His teachers were unfamiliar with the notion, and told us that living in two homes was not a good idea. It was important for us to educate the educators and communicate with them about what joint custody was like for our son. Now that joint custody is more common, most teachers have some awareness about the benefits and difficulties inherent in the plan.

We've had two experiences with teachers, one positive and one negative. Ethan's first-grade teacher was very understanding of our needs as co-parents. She made sure that school announcements were sent to both of us. She knew Ethan's schedule, and she was very aware of our situation. It made going to parent-teacher conferences a real pleasure for me and Kate.

The second-grade teacher was not at all accepting of Ethan's living arrangements. One time she asked the kids to draw pictures of their families, and Ethan started drawing two different houses with us and our new assorted family members in each house. When he got negative feedback from the teacher about the picture, he changed it totally. He drew a picture of me and Kate with himself in the middle holding hands with each of us; there was a house, one house, in the background with smoke rings coming out of the chimney. He figured out what the teacher wanted, and he did it. Of course, it had no relationship at all to Ethan's reality. [Ronald]

People who are unfamiliar with joint custody might feel intimidated or puzzled by it. In general, any new ideas about

. . . .

raising children seem to arouse opposition. It might be hard for people who are not close to the situation to imagine how children could live in two homes. Others might feel threatened because they are staying in their own marriages "for the sake of the children" and don't want to examine the real reasons for staying together.

At times I felt that people were watching Josh very closely for negative effects of co-parenting. In addition, people observed the interactions between Josh, Jeff, and me. Not necessarily critical of us, they were interested in our so-called experiment, our small version of the Brave New World. Sometimes I didn't mind people's curiosity, and other times it felt uncomfortable and irritating. Josh, on the other hand, seemed oblivious to people's scrutiny of us. He did not experience this as a problem of joint custody. Indeed, it is important to distinguish between the challenges joint custody presents to parents and to children. As far as Josh was concerned, he was just living his life, having fun most of the time, being upset sometimes, doing whatever children do.

Family members, as well as friends, react to joint custody in ways that may cause difficulties for co-parents. Women who share parenting often feel that they are being criticized for not being proper mothers when they are willing to "let" their ex-husbands "have" the children for a few days a week. This attitude implies that children are property to give or keep. What kind of mother would agree to be without her children for three days every week? Surely there is something strange about her. Men, on the other hand, are often not taken seriously as parents, even when they share all responsibility with their ex-wives for childrearing. From this perspective, co-parenting fathers are seen as rather strange themselves. What kind of man would choose to do "women's work?"

My mother-in-law was dead set against co-parenting at first. Now she sees that I'm home a great deal of the time with my kids, and she's envious. No one was home with her, and her husband didn't

*participate in raising their kids. I think the older generation is
admiring, but they're not quite sure what the cost of it is. A lot of
it is in their attitudes about men: "If you're a real man you'd be
out there earning a living, and if you're sharing custody it means
you're not quite fully responsible in some ways." Yet there's an
admiration at the same time—something about it being tough to be
a man who is doing a woman's work.* [Evan]

In the beginning months of my joint-custody arrangement, my
parents had difficulty adjusting. My mother felt that Josh should
be with me all the time. She had trouble understanding that I
didn't have the freedom to come to her house with Josh for a
weekend at a moment's notice. I needed to plan such a trip with
Jeff in advance, yet she didn't feel that Jeff's days with Josh were
important for me to consider. Over the years, as my parents have
seen my unwillingness, indeed inability, to have Josh for full
weekends without making arrangements with Jeff, the pressure I
have felt from them to do this has decreased. For them it meant
that they did not have constant access to Josh. They, too, had to
learn what Josh's schedule was and where they would be able to
find him on which days.

When I wrote the first edition of this book, this is what my
mother had to say about joint custody:

*Today's children seem to have the remarkable facility of rolling
with the punches and adjusting to crazy situations. Where genuine
love and interest in Josh is evident, he seems to accept almost any
arrangement and not suffer any apparent ill effects. But I can't
help wishing he led a less complicated life, uncluttered by the need
for endless arrangements. Josh is a delightful seven-year-old to
have around—bright, loving, and articulate. When he is with us,
on infrequent but wonderful visits, we love him to pieces, but our
pain is there and we worry. What grandparents wouldn't?*

Now, 13 years later, my mother sees her grandson as a well-adjusted and resourceful young adult. "After the initial period of adjustment," says my mother, "the arrangements seemed like second nature to him. He had school, friends, and other activities which were primary. What I don't like is that I never get to see him—he's too busy!" Spoken like a true grandmother!

Another grandmother I know expressed these thoughts about co-parenting:

When my son and daughter-in-law first told me of their separation, I was crestfallen—but my first concern was for my darling six-year-old granddaughter.

Then, about the time I felt I was adjusting to their separation, they hit me with another mind blower! They were going to have joint custody, or do co-parenting, both of which were new terms to me. My son explained that my granddaughter would live with him for half the week and her mother for the other half. Well, I hit the ceiling! I ranted and raved and said it would be terrible for our granddaughter—being split up like that. She would have no feeling of roots. We argued about it, but they stood firm. My husband and I were heartbroken. We didn't believe it could work.

But I am pleased to say we were wrong. We see positive things happening. Because of their new arrangement, our son and his daughter have become closer to each other than when they all lived together. He really has to take full charge in the absence of her mother. Also, seeing each parent alone has given the child the opportunity to know them as individuals, not just as a parental unit. [Yetta]

Grandparents can be a tremendous resource to your children in time of uncertainty and loss. In *Surviving the Breakup*, Wallerstein and Kelly noted that children of divorce "who had extended families, especially grandparents, who were close by or who kept up a continuing interest from a distance, were very much helped by this support system." Sometimes it is difficult for families who have joint custody to continue relationships with both sets of grandparents. For example, a mother who feels animosity toward her ex-in-laws might not welcome their involvement with her children. Although a father can take responsibility for these contacts, a mother is in a position to encourage or discourage these relationships. If grandparents are pulled into taking sides in a divorce, the situation becomes very strained, and they are less able to provide their grandchildren with a supportive, nurturing relationship.

In *Grandparents/Grandchildren—The Vital Connection*, Arthur Kornhaber and Kenneth L. Woodward encourage grandparents to be "guardians of the young" and advise them "to let everyone in the family know that they have you to rely on in a family emergency." Divorce is one such emergency. Although it may be difficult for you to tell your parents and your in-laws that your marriage is over, your children could use extra support from both sets of grandparents.

When faced with criticisms of joint custody from friends and family, the more secure you are about your parenting plan, the less vulnerable you will feel and the less open to criticism. Although it is easy to get swept away by other people's doubts, you can use those doubts as a stimulus for yourself to reconsider: is joint custody a plan that is working for you and your family? *Your* answer is the one that matters.

Divorce brings with it anxiety and guilt about the children. Joint custody can increase this anxiety if you are not certain that this parenting plan is 100 percent right for your children. If you are structuring new ways of relating to your children, you will face difficulties such as being without your children some of the time, adjusting the schedule to meet their needs, negotiating with your ex-spouse, handling reactions from teachers, family, and friends, and resolving your own feelings about the divorce.

Conflicts are inherent in any plan for childrearing after divorce. Joint custody provides a structure for both parents to maintain an intimate relationship with their children. In addition, mothers are freer to develop their own individual, adult interests, while fathers can rearrange their priorities to spend more time with their children.

The challenge is to help your children adjust to a life that no parent would have chosen for them—living separately with each parent. In the beginning, especially, this requires a lot of hard work. There are rewards, however, and they come in the form of loving, close relationships between both parents and their children.

9

The Future

Joint custody is not a panacea. It's an arrangement. It's
what people do with it that makes it successful
or not.   —Elaine Smith, Philadelphia attorney
                                    specializing in family law

Public understanding and acceptance of joint custody has gone
through several stages. In the early 1970s, joint custody was seen as
an unhealthy way to raise children. Then, in the early 1980s, joint
custody was seen as the wave of the future. State legislatures
responded by enacting joint-custody laws, and a new group of joint-
custody families appeared—ones ordered by the courts. Now, in the
1990s, we are seeing a swing away from joint custody and back to
custody arrangements that favor the primary caregiver, the preferred
arrangement for most of the twentieth century. Why the shift?

Building on Experience

Joint custody is an ideal. Some children and parents have done well with shared parenting plans. Almost invariably, parents who succeed agree to the arrangement voluntarily, sometimes with the help of a trained mediator. They are able to escape a bitter custody dispute and an extended battle over the property settlement. They are usually middle class, well educated, and have comfortable incomes. In many, but certainly not all of these families, little if any money changes hands, except for major expenses like medical care or tuition costs. Rather, each parent has assumed the costs of caring for the children when they are with them. In addition, these parents have been sensitive to their children's changing needs and have been flexible in working out new parenting plans. If they are not on friendly or neutral terms, they have at least been able to put their bitterness aside so they can talk to each other and cooperate in raising their children. The children, too, have been flexible and have adapted to living in two homes. They can keep their schedules straight and may even thrive because of the attention they get from both parents and from the diversity in their lives. What matters most to them is that they haven't lost either parent because of the divorce.

Unfortunately, these families seem to be in the minority. More typical is the family in which bitterness and rancor still dominate the parents' relationship and the children are caught in the middle of their parents' continuing struggles. The children are aware of the tension and know their parents have a hard time speaking with each other. When joint custody has been awarded by the court over one parent's objection (and sometimes over both parents' objection) and the antagonism toward the parenting plan persists, it is unlikely to be satisfying for any family member.

Sam Kirschner, Ph.D., family therapist and co-author of *Comprehensive Family Therapy*, believes that joint custody should only be awarded to the mentally mature, or those who have been able to go through divorce in a mature way. People who display immaturity—those who are unwilling to compromise and cooperate—are not good candidates for joint custody. Getting a divorce is not a sign of immaturity, but how the individuals behave throughout the process of the divorce is a good measure. If an immature couple turns to a judge to determine their parenting plan, that judge should "steer them away from joint custody or else it will be a nightmare," says Kirschner.

As the general public has gained more knowledge of an experience with joint custody, it seems that men and women have focused their criticisms differently. Sheila James Kuehl, the Managing Attorney of the Southern California Women's Law Center and an Associate Professor of Law at Loyola University Law School in Los Angeles says, "Simply put, joint custody is a gender issue. Fathers fight for it. Women, mothers and advocates, as well as advocates for children, fight against it." Women who focus on the gender issue argue that fathers fight for joint custody as a bargaining chip. The ultimate prize for these fathers is a reduction in the amount of child support they have to pay. Often, these fathers are not serious about wanting to be involved with the children. Some are serious, however, about wanting to harass their ex-wives and exercising some control in a situation in which they feel they have none. According to Gary Skoloff, chairman of the Family Law Section of the American Bar Association, most fathers want good visitation rights. For the most part, men want to continue the system of parenting already established in their marriage, in which the mother is the primary caretaker. They do not want the responsibility of caring for a sick child, taking children to piano lessons, and so on.

Kuehl points out that "custody battles are really an argument over who gets control and men especially react badly to having the sense of control taken away."

Beverly Webster Ferreiro, Ph.D., Associate Clinical Professor in the School of Nursing at the University of North Carolina at Chapel Hill, believes that there is an advantage to using the label of joint custody, because "one parent is not symbolically wounded or disenfranchised." The label often has nothing to do with what happens in practice, but there is still a powerful association attached to it.

The power that joint custody confers to fathers is what angers many mothers and women's rights advocates. Dr. Deborah Luepnitz, a family therapist affiliated with Philadelphia Child Guidance Clinic, says she now sees too many cases in which the court awards joint custody for the parent who can afford the court battle—most often the father. Mothers are often afraid to contest joint custody, fearing that they will appear hostile and uncooperative, and will lose custody altogether.

Dr. Marla Isaacs, co-author of *The Difficult Divorce*, says that many people have joint custody simply because they assume they must. She notes, "When a husband wants joint custody or the husband's lawyer tells him to want it, on what grounds can a woman refuse these days? That is inviting litigation." Dr. Isaacs believes that joint custody has not helped women in general. She says that women are perceived as being selfish if they want to be with their children full time. In other words, they feel pressured into letting the father have the children part of the time. Women also experience a great deal of anxiety in participating in a joint-custody situation. If the father remarries (which constitutes a change of circumstances) and sues for full custody, the mother may fear that her former husband's home will look like the more stable or normal one, and that she will lose all custody rights.

In 1983, Joanne Schulman, staff attorney for the National Center on Women, said that "joint custody is being used to hold women hostage." Other women point out that joint custody puts mothers or children who have been abused in a most untenable situation. "Mothers, for example, who try to prove that their ex-husbands are molesting their children probably face a much tougher legal battle in those jurisdictions which encourage equalized parenting after divorce," says Dr. Diane Trombetta. Women who have been abused are often terrified of negotiating with their ex-husbands, and it is likely that any agreement entered into by an abused mother is one into which she has been coerced.

On the positive side, joint-custody arrangements can provide women with opportunities for self-actualization. Some women who are divorcing still want more for themselves than full-time motherhood can provide. They want to expand their horizons beyond the role of motherhood. Joint custody provides many women the freedom to devote their child-free time to their work lives. They plan their schedules so that long days and evening meetings coincide with times they are not responsible for their children.

While joint custody has evolved out of a broader movement of social change, the experience that many families have had with this new family form over the years has been anything but satisfying. The women's movement of the late 1960s and early 1970s created an atmosphere in which the dynamics of male-female relationships were explored and traditional role expectations were questioned.

Men who began to take more responsibility for childcare and household tasks within their marriage found great satisfaction in being nurturers of their children. They called into question some assumptions they had about the role of a career or job in their lives. They felt their need to maintain a sense of family in whatever kind of family structure exists, and they saw that being sensitive fathers was not incongruous with their manhood.

Women sharing economic responsibilities and men sharing childrearing and household maintenance responsibilities constitutes an upheaval in traditional family roles. Most women who are presently staying home to raise young children will, and want to, return to work outside the home in the future. Economics, as well as a need for personal fulfillment, dictates this trend. Men who participate in their children's lives derive a great deal of personal satisfaction from their involvement.

With all these changes, the traditional family model—in which mom takes care of the house and the children and dad earns the money—is still the most predominant. After divorce, the traditional custody arrangement, in which mom gets the house and the children and dad has visitation privileges—is still the most prevalent.

And a new study by Frank Furstenberg and Kathleen Mullan Harris, both of the University of Pennsylvania, has shown that there is a new phenomenon that appears after divorce: "the disappearing American father, who leaves his children, emotionally and financially." Families representing different races, geographic locations, income and educational levels were studied, with alarmingly similar results. Millions of American children have no contact with their fathers whatsoever, and for millions more, contact with their fathers is minimal.

"Men regard marriage as a package deal," says Furstenberg. "They cannot separate their relations with their children from their relations to their former spouse. When that relationship ends, the paternal bond usually withers within a few years, too."

For the minority of men who choose to co-parent, they have the experience of developing a side of themselves that normal socialization patterns have tended to inhibit. These men talk about discovering a tender side of themselves that comes from being with their children. The man responding to his child's emotional needs satisfies a part of himself that is longing for connection and intimacy.

A child's love is unconditional. It is pure and unique in that respect. Too many men miss having that experience. It isn't the same as adult love—it isn't what you get or want or need from the love of an adult. It is its own special thing. You can live without it, but it is very, very special to experience it. [Jeff]

For the minority of men who choose to co-parent, their relationship with their children improves. These are the men who really want to share parenting responsibilities with their ex-spouses. They note that as soon as they moved out of the house they experienced an improvement. For some it has meant leaving behind a household full of the tension of the deteriorating marital relationship. For others, it has been an opportunity to work out their own rhythms with their children. And for others it has meant becoming secure in their own ability to parent.

American society places a premium on motherhood as the best means for raising children. As a result, most men feel inadequate to the task, and never realize their potential as fathers. . . . Being alone with Julie has meant all these things to me and many more. Now, when I look at Julie, she seems so happy and in such great shape. I realize that I must be doing something right. I have learned how important I am to Julie and how important she is to me. [Jim]

Everyday acts have repercussions in the social system, repercussions we cannot fully realize. A father who is involved in his child's schooling, for instance, will create a different pattern of teacher-parent interaction, which will in turn affect teacher-student interaction. A father who tells his work colleagues that he cannot be at an early evening meeting because he has responsibilities for his children will stimulate their thinking in a new way. They will be forced to recognize that taking care of the children is of major importance to this father. His voice is that of the minority, perhaps, but it will be heard. Any step in a new and different direction will stir people; they might be threatened, surprised, supportive, antagonistic—but there will be some reaction.

There are times when I've said to my colleagues that they shouldn't have meetings between 5:30 and 7:30 p.m. because that's hard on parents. They just assume that anyone can meet at any time and that you have your slave at home to take care of the kids. Or you should get a sitter and it doesn't matter if it's the first day that your kid is coming back to you. The kind of life I'm living doesn't mean that I do less work or qualitatively less good work. It does mean that I have to set things up differently and that I need help in doing that. [Steve]

Joint custody forces you to interact with the social system in ways that you may not anticipate. Because you are doing something unusual, you find yourself in a position of needing to educate people, talking about what you do and why you do it, and examining your own feelings about your parenting plan.

What are my feelings about the unknown and the future? Well, when Austin is with his mother I don't know what's happening there, and I've learned to trust that. Thinking about fear, about what's going to happen to the children when they grow up, is fear of the unknown and fear of the time when you no longer have control of every aspect of your kid's life. And I think co-parenting prepares you for that eventuality because you have a regular experience of trusting things that you don't know about, of trusting when you don't know what's going on. [Harvey]

Social changes that have resulted from the increasing divorce rate and the need to create new parenting plans are ongoing. New configurations will emerge, ones that we have not begun to address. One new family form involves gay and lesbian parents. I have worked with several families in which the parents have divorced and one of the parents is gay and now living with a lover. The children move back and forth between two homes with two very distinct lifestyles. Some of these children, especially adolescents, find it extremely difficult to be faced with such conflicting forces in their lives. Some cannot accept their parents' gay lifestyle, while others seem to have made peace with it, accept it, and can be open about it with their friends.

Another new family form is composed of two women who choose to raise a child together in one home and share parenting with the child's father. An example are the lovers Carol and Mona. Mona had a child from a previous marriage, and Carol wanted a child as well. She asked her friend Warren to impregnate her, which he did. Derek was born, and was primarily raised by Carol and Mona, with infrequent visits from his long-distance father. In time, Carol and Mona separated and Warren began to take a more active interest in his son. Carol and Mona share the major childraising responsibilities for Derek from two separate homes. Warren, who lives several hundred miles away, visits Derek whenever he can.

Growing Up Together

Recent research has suggested that most children of divorce have a very difficult time adjusting to their new family lifestyles, and that the custodial arrangement itself is not the critical factor in how well children fare. Rather, it seems the postdivorce relationship between parents sets the tone for how well the children fare. The age and sex of the child and the overall satisfaction the parents have with the parenting plan also affect children's postdivorce adjustment.

Research findings about the long-term negative effects of divorce on children will force parents to look closely at the arrangements they have created. Have joint-custody parents developed a plan in which, in effect, they have both abdicated responsibility? When both parents have to make joint decisions concerning the welfare of their children and the parents disagree, no decision gets made. No decision, that is, until either one parent gets worn down or a judge decides.

For children, joint custody can have a very special influence on their upbringing. Indeed, they may have more of their parents' individual time and attention than most children do. They have seen that their parents, while no longer living together, maintain a major commitment to parenting and to being available to them in a complete sense. They are likely to experience an expanded range of activities and to have relationships with a greater number of caring adults than they would if they were in a more traditional custody arrangement.

As my son said when he was seven,

You get to know more people, 'cause your dad has a lot of friends and your mom has a lot of friends. Otherwise you would just know who your dad and your mom know together. And you get to go more different places than you would if you were one whole family. [Josh]

Many joint-custody children work at seeing the positives in their situation. One young girl told me, "I have one home twice. I take the best of each and mush it together."

Children growing up in joint custody know that many options and many solutions lie within the realm of possibility. They know that some people may view the way they live as unusual, although to them it feels ordinary. Joint-custody children whose parents have learned to cooperate see that it is possible to divorce and not hate an ex-spouse. Their own horizons are broadened about how adult relationships can be managed. They learn at an impressionable age that life is not a matter of either/or choices and black/white issues, but that life involves flexibility and constant adjustments. And they learn that people can make choices about their lives and have control over how they live.

The other day someone called; my daughter, who is nine, answered the phone. Someone asked for her mother. She said, "My mother's not here, my parents are divorced, and if you'd like to talk to her, I can give you her phone number." She handled it so smoothly. It was a real clear awareness of the reality, with no emotional connection to that reality. [Geoffrey]

Children whose parents have separated and divorced certainly know that life holds surprises for them and that they are able to adjust to new situations as they arise. They can look back at times that were difficult for them and see that they have managed to make it through, and that they have changed and grown through it all.

Ex-spouses, too, can learn from the divorce process. Initially, there are anxious, angry times when it seems impossible to have civil conversation, and some parents never progress beyond this point. But many do. They learn that although they have gotten a divorce on paper, really, they can never divorce each other—that is, they can never say they want nothing more to do with the other— because they are parents of the same children. At one point in their lives, they chose each other to be a parent to their children. That bears remembering. What was good about this person? What attracted you to this person? Is there anything left of that appeal that could now be used to enhance cooperative parenting? Some parents have come to enjoy, appreciate and respect their ex-spouse. My ex-husband and I are more to each other than Josh's parents. We have been friends now for 25 years with the exception of a few tense years immediately following our separation. We benefit from our relationship in a way that is not only related to Josh, but is also very clearly related to our appreciation and respect for each other as people who were once married. Our lives have been enhanced in this way, and so has Josh's.

There was a time, not too long ago, when the intact family was seen as the only environment in which to raise emotionally healthy children. In recent years, we have learned not to romanticize the ideal of the nuclear family. We also know that it is not helpful to romanticize or idealize the notion of joint custody. It takes a lot of dedication, commitment, and hard work to provide emotionally safe environments for our children in various kinds of living situations. Joint custody, with parents sharing their children equally, is one such kind.

Life provides us with ongoing opportunities to have interchanges that are either satisfying or dissatisfying, destructive or constructive. With an ex-spouse, there are endless situations that test our ability to be cooperative, yes, for the sake of the children. Mothers and fathers want to provide their children with love and warmth, affection and fun. But they also want to live their own lives to the fullest. After separation or divorce, joint custody, agreed to voluntarily by two mature adults, provides a dynamic, effective way to make that happen.

As we look toward the future for new models of family living, naturally we wonder how our present parenting arrangements will affect our children. We can plan for the future, but we cannot foresee the final outcome. As co-parents, we cannot predict what kind of adults our children will become; no parents can. We can only hope that if we provide our children with large doses of understanding, support, and affection—and keep our marital squabbles out of the range of co-operative parenting—then our children will be all right.

Suggested Readings

These books are recommended for further general reading. A list of additional works, including professional sources, may be found in the Bibliography.

Books for Children

Bienenfeld, Florence. *My Mom and Dad Are Getting a Divorce!* St. Paul, Minnesota: EMC Publishing, 1984.

Brown, Laurene Krasny and Marc Brown. *Dinosaurs Divorce: A Guide for Changing Families*. Boston: Little, Brown & Company, 1986.

Gardner, Richard A. *The Boys and Girls Book About Divorce*. New York: Bantam Books, 1971.

Krementz, Jill. *How It Feels When Parents Divorce*. New York: Alfred A. Knopf, 1988.

Rofes, Eric, editor. *The Kids' Book of Divorce: By, For & About Kids*. New York: Vintage Books, 1982.

Books for Parents

Adler, Robert E. *Sharing the Children: How to Resolve Custody Problems and Get On with Your Life*. Bethesda, MD: Adler & Adler, 1988.

Ahrons, Constance R. and Roy H. Rodgers. *Divorced Families: A Multidisciplinary View*. New York: W.W. Norton, 1987.

Burns, Cherie. *Stepmotherhood: How to Survive Without Feeling Frustrated, Left Out or Wicked*. New York: Times Books, 1985.

Chesler, Phyllis. *Mothers on Trial: The Battle for Children and Custody*. Seattle: Seal Press, 1986.

Cohen, Miriam Galper. *Long Distance Parenting: A Guide for Divorced Parents*. New York: New American Library, 1989.

Einstein, Elizabeth. *The Stepfamily: Living, Loving & Learning*. Boston: Shambhala Publications, Inc., 1985.

Ferrara, Frank. *On Being Father: A Divorced Man Talks About Sharing the New Responsibilities of Parenthood*. New York: Doubleday & Co., 1985.

Fisher, Roger and William Ury. *Getting To Yes: Negotiating Agreement Without Giving In*. New York: Penguin Books, 1981.

SUGGESTED READINGS

Folberg, Jay, editor. *Joint Custody and Shared Parenting*. The Bureau of National Affairs Inc., 1984.

Gardner, Richard A. *The Parent's Book About Divorce*. New York: Bantam Books, 1980.

Greif, Geoffrey L. and Mary S. Pabst. *Mothers Without Custody*. Lexington, Mass: Lexington Books, 1982.

Isaacs, Marla Beth, Braulio Montalvo and David Abelsohn. *The Difficult Divorce: Therapy for Children and Families*. New York: Basic Books, Inc., 1986.

Kornhaber, Arthur, and Kenneth L. Woodward. *Grandparents/ Grandchildren: The Vital Connection*. New York: Anchor Press, 1981.

Lansky, Vicki. *Vicki Lansky's Divorce Book for Parents*. New York: New American Library, 1989.

Newman, George. *101 Ways to Be a Long Distance Super-Dad*. Mountain View, California: Blossom Valley Press, 1984.

Osherson, Samuel. *Finding Our Fathers: The Unfinished Business of Manhood*. New York: The Free Press, 1986.

Paskowicz, Patricia. *Absentee Mothers*. New York: Universe Books, 1982

Ricci, Isolina. *Mom's House, Dad's House: Making Shared Custody Work*. New York: Macmillan Publishing Co., 1980.

Roman, Mel and William Haddad. *The Disposable Parent*. New York: Holt, Rhinehart and Winston, 1978.

Roosevelt, Ruth and Jeannette Lofas. *Living in Step: A Remarriage Manual for Parents and Children*. New York: McGraw Hill, 1976.

Rosin, Mark Bruce. *Stepfathering*. New York: Ballantine Books, 1987.

Virtue, Doreen. *My Kids Don't Live with Me Anymore*. Minneapolis: CompCare Publishers, 1988.

Visher, Emily B. and John S. Visher. *How to Win As a Stepfamily*. New York: Dember Books, 1982.

Wallerstein, Judith S. and Sandra Blakeslee. *Second Chances: Men, Women & Children a Decade After Divorce*. New York: Ticknor & Fields, 1989.

Wallerstein, Judith S. and Joan Berlin Kelly. *Surviving the Breakup: How Children and Parents Cope with Divorce*. New York: Basic Books, Inc., 1980.

Ware, Ciji. *Sharing Parenthood After Divorce*. New York: Viking Press, 1982.

Woolley, Persia. *The Custody Handbook*. New York: Summit Books, 1979.

Resources

Academy of Family Mediators
P.O. Box 10501
Eugene, OR 97440
(503) 345-1205
Call or write for information regarding mediators and mediation
services.

American Association for Marriage and Family Therapy
1100 17th Street, N.W., 10th floor
Washington, D.C. 20036
(202) 452-0109
Call or write for listings of marriage and family therapists in
your area.

Association of Family and Conciliation Courts
329 W. Wilson Street
Madison, WI 53703
(608) 251–4001
This association publishes an excellent brochure on joint custody as well as a journal with the most current thinking on joint custody.

Fathers' and Children's Equality (FACE)
P.O. Box 117
Drexel Hill, PA 19026
(215) 688–4748
There are local FACE chapters throughout the country.

Joint Custody Association
10606 Wilkins Avenue
Los Angeles, CA 90024
(213) 475–5352
James A. Cook, President

Mothers Without Custody
P.O. Box 27418
Houston, TX 77227–7418
(404) 662–8020
Support groups exist in different parts of the country.

Parents Without Partners
8807 Colesville Road
Silver Spring, MD 20910
(301) 588–9354

Stepfamily Association of America, Inc.
215 Centennial Mall South, Suite 212
Lincoln, NE 68508
(402) 477–STEP
This organization publishes a quarterly bulletin and a booklet of educational resources for stepfamilies and professionals.

Bibliography

Abarbanel, Alice. "Shared Parenting After Separation and Divorce: A Study of Joint Custody." *American Journal of Orthopsychiatry* 49 (1979).

Atkin, Edith, and Estelle Rubin. *Part-time Father.* New York: New American Library, 1976.

Baum, Charlotte. "The Best of Both Parents." *The New York Times Magazine* (October 31, 1976).

Bohannon, Paul. "The Six Stations of Divorce." *Divorce and After.* New York: Doubleday and Company, 1970.

Clingempeel, W. Glenn, and N. Dickon Repucci. "Joint Custody

After Divorce: Major Issues and Goals for Research." Psychological Bulletin 9 (1982).

Ferreiro, Beverly Webster. "Presumption of Joint Custody: A Family Policy Dilemma." *Journal of Family Relations* 39 (October, 1990).

Folberg, Jay. "Joint Custody Law—The Second Wave." *Journal of Family Law* 23 (1984–85).

Gardner, Richard A. *Family Evaluation in Child Custody Litigation*. Creskill, New Jersey: Creative Therapeutics, 1982.

———. "My Involvement in Child Custody Litigation: Past, Present and Future." *Family and Conciliation Courts Review* 27 (July, 1989).

Glazer, Sarah. "Joint Custody: Is It Good for Children?" *Editorial Research Reports* 1 (February 3, 1989).

Goldstein, Joseph; Anna Freud; Albert Solnit. *Beyond the Best Interests of the Child*. New York: The Free Press, 1973.

Greif, Judith Brown. "Fathers, Children and Joint Custody." *American Journal of Orthopsychiatry* 49 (1979).

Hess, R.D., and K.A. Camara. "Post-divorce Family Relationships as Mediating Factors in the Consequences of Divorce for Children." *Journal of Social Issues* 35 (1979).

Hetherington, E. Mavis. "Divorced Fathers." *The Family Coordinator* 25 (October, 1976).

Hollandsworth, Marla. Testimony to the House Judiciary Committee of Maryland Regarding Joint Custody of

Children. "In Opposition to HB 501, HB 753, HB 1116." March 3, 1983.

Holly, Marcia. "Joint Custody: The New Haven Plan." *Ms.*, September, 1976.

Johnston, J.R.; M. Kline; J.M. Tschann; L.E.G. Campbell. "Ongoing Post-Divorce Conflict in Families Contesting Custody: Does Joint Custody and Frequent Access Help?" Paper presented at the 65th annual meeting of the American Orthopsychiatric Association. March 30, 1988.

Kirschner, Sam, and Diana Adile Kirschner. *Comprehensive Family Therapy.* New York: Brunner/Mazel, 1986.

Kuehl, Sheila James. "Against Joint Custody: A Dissent to the General Bullmoose Theory." *Family and Conciliation Courts Review* 27 (December, 1989).

Lewin, Tamar. "Father's Vanishing Act Called Common Drama." *The New York Times.* June 4, 1990.

Luepnitz, Deborah. *Child Custody: A Study of Families After Divorce.* Lexington, Mass.: Lexington Books, 1982.

McKinnon, Rosemary, and Judith S. Wallerstein. "A Preventive Intervention Program for Parents and Young Children in Joint Custody Arrangements." *American Journal of Orthopsychiatry* 58 (1988).

Ricci, Isolina. "Mediation, Joint Custody and Legal Agreements: A Time to Review, Revise and Refine. *Family and Conciliation Courts Review* 27 (July, 1989).

Rosen, Paula. "A Study of Joint Custody Families." Ph.D. diss., Bryn Mawr College, 1982.

Smullens, SaraKay Cohen. "The Trouble with Joint Custody." *The Legal Intelligencer* 200 (June 28, 1989).

———. [as SaraKay Cohen]. *Whoever Said Life Is Fair? A Guide to Growing Through Life's Injustices*. New York: Scribners, 1980.

Stahl, Philip M. "A Review of Joint and Shared Parenting Literature." Edited by J. Folberg. The Bureau of National Affairs, Inc., 1984.

Steinman, Susan. "The Experience of Children in a Joint Custody Arrangement: A Report of a Study." *American Journal of Orthopsychiatry* 51 (1981).

Ware, Ciji. "What a Mediator Can Do." *Ms*. April, 1983.

Index

About the Author

Miriam Galper Cohen is a family therapist in private practice in Philadelphia who specializes in working with families in transition. She holds a Master of Science in Social Work from Columbia University, is a clinical member of the American Association for Marriage and Family Therapy, and is a member of the National Association of Social Workers and the Academy of Certified Social Workers. She has acted as an expert witness in child-custody cases and has testified before state judiciary committees investigating joint custody. She resides in Glenside, Pennsylvania.

Other books by the author include *Long Distance Parenting: A Guide for Divorced Parents* (New American Library, 1989) and (as a contributing writer) *Women in Transition: A Feminist Handbook on Separation and Divorce* (Scribners, 1975).